THE STUFFED OWL

Statesman of Olden Time, making without wish for emolument a flat but faithful version of the Georgics, in English hexameters

THE STUFFED OWL

AN ANTHOLOGY OF BAD VERSE

SELECTED AND ARRANGED
BY D. B. WYNDHAM LEWIS
AND CHARLES LEE

★

WITH EIGHT CARTOONS
FROM THE WORKS OF
MAX BEERBOHM

★

Yet, helped by Genius—untired Comforter,
The presence even of a stuffed Owl for her
Can cheat the time.   [WORDSWORTH.

LONDON
J. M. DENT AND SONS LIMITED

PREFACE

Video meliora proboque,
Deteriora sequor.
        OVID, METAM., VII, 20.

We scan and approve of the better,
    We go for the worse.

PREFACE

A CERTAIN delicacy, which the most abandoned reader will hardly dare to flout, or the most fastidious presume to improbate, excludes from these pages many honoured names of the present moment. It is highly possible that more than one admirer of modern English Verse having read thus far will dash this modest volume at once to the book-shop floor, crying derisively that one might as well pay for admission to South Kensington to find the glass cases full of dead mice and little bits of string, and turning thence with a scowl to spend his six shillings instead on Mr. Tweet's new historical drama in verse—a course we think unwise. To such critics we would simply appeal in the words of Pope:

> But if in noble Minds some Dregs remain,
> Not yet purg'd off, of Spleen and sour Disdain,
> Discharge that Rage on more provoking Crimes—

for in the compilers' estimation the enrichment of this book (not to speak of its considerable enlargement) with extracts from eminent living English poets would not compensate the momentary hot embarrassment all round which would perhaps have followed our request to Mr. Boom, Mr. Tweet, Mr. Blandish, Mrs. Henry Bodnick, and the others for permission to quote from their works. It was realised that although the majority of these leading poets would not hesitate, probably, to point out to us with the greatest affability portions of their own verse suitable to our purpose, they would be quick to resent any sort of slighting criticism of the work of their *chers Maîtres et confrères*. The half-formed plan was therefore rejected,

> for Time shall first expire,
> Ere JOHNSON stay, when Virtue bids retire,

and we do not doubt that this resolution will when all is said and done be applauded alike by the thoughtful, the pious, and the genteel.

It would seem at a hasty glance that to make an anthology of Bad Verse is on the whole a simple matter—a matter, say, of skimming lightly through one or two of the principal existing anthologies of English Verse, making a quick but judicious selection, adding a few official and semi-official performances on topics of Imperial moment — the Diamond Jubilee, the relief of Mafeking, Derby Day, the White City, Selfridge's extension, the Great War—with others plucked from the columns of this or that national Organ of Opinion, sprinkling in a few extracts from those slim and dainty green- or grey - bound volumes published almost continuously at the author's charge (and not forgetting the stouter epic volumes of the Yorkshire gentleman who describes himself as "The Modern Homer"), and deftly mingling with these in one harmonious whole some of the verse with which the Muse has been known to inspire our brethren and cousins overseas to celebrate love, war, or some outstanding financial merger.

On the contrary. *Distinguo.* Bad Verse has its canons, like Good Verse. There is bad Bad Verse and good Bad Verse. It has been the constant preoccupation of the compilers to include in this book chiefly good Bad Verse. The field of bad Bad Verse is vast, and confusing in its tropical luxuriance. The illiterate, the semi-literate, the Babu, the nature-loving contributor to the county newspaper, the retired station - master, the spinster lady coyly attuned to Life and Spring, the hearty but ill-equipped patriot, the pudibond yet urgent Sapphos of endless *Keepsakes* and *Lady's Magazines* — nearly all those amateurs, inapt for commerce with the Nine, who have ever attempted Parnassus (that is, about one-tenth of the average annual population of Empire) have been passed over, often with reluctance; for good Bad Verse is grammatical, it is constructed according to the Rubrics, its rhythms, rimes, and metres are impeccable. A rough illustration of the distinction will readily occur. Bad Bad Verse is a strong but inexperienced female child doggedly attacking Debussy's *Fêtes* in a remote provincial suburb on a hire-payment pianoforte from the Swiftsure Furnishing Stores. Good Bad Verse is Rummel or Lamond executing *Warblings at Eve* at Queen's Hall on a Bechstein concert-grand.

It would seem necessary, before going further, to warn the reader strongly against despising or patronising good Bad Verse. There is no greater mistake. "My dear friend," as Dr. Johnson said to Boswell, "clear your *mind* of cant. You may *talk* in this manner; it is a mode of talking in Society: but don't *think* foolishly." It would, indeed, be a permissible exercise in dialectic to prove here con-clusively and inclusively, if we had the time, that good Bad Verse has an eerie, supernal beauty com-parable in its accidents with the beauty of Good

Verse.   Rémy de Gourmont dealt effectively in the late nineties with a certain brutish type of Classical Don who—he is perennial—is moved by bigotry to deny the literary eminence of certain liturgical Latin poetry, the *Pange Lingua*, the *Lauda Sion* ("*ces vers de bronze*").   There may be similar Grobians in existence who would attempt to argue, for example, that the cathedrals of Chartres and Burgos and Seville and Beauvais and Ely are " inferior " to the Parthenon: such primary suburban stuff will be appraised at its worth by the man of taste.   But one must not strain analogies too far.   We will merely assert here that good Bad Verse (which may henceforth be understood as the kind with which this book is principally concerned) is devilish pleasing.

It remains—the axiom being established that Bad Verse of the good kind is innocent of faults of craftsmanship—to be suggested what makes it bad.   This quality is not easy to define in one phrase, for as all the delicate tints of the prism, softly glowing and changing and melting one into the other, unite to form the perfect opal, so do many exquisite *nuances* of badness unite to make Bad Verse.   The most obvious and predominating tint, of course, is bathos: that sudden slip and swoop and slither as down a well-buttered slide, from the peaks into the abyss.   When some dignified, headline personage, an eminent Academic, a gaitered Divine, an important Actor - Manager, a leading Thinker, a prominent Financier, skids on a scrap of banana-peel in the street and suddenly presents his western façade to the shuddering stars, the impact on the sensations of a thoughtful observer is more tremendous than if the exercise had been performed by a nobody, some urchin, some shabby man of letters, some threadbare saint. Similarly, it is generally the most distinguished poets who provide the nicest Bad Verse—and by "distinguished" we mean here poets who, whether great in the absolute sense or otherwise, have been rewarded with reverence and royalties by their contemporaries. Thus Wordsworth; thus Robert Montgomery; thus Tennyson; thus Eliza Cook. The more eminent the poet the more imposing the glissade, the more shattering the bump below. When Samuel Johnson, Pontifex Maximus, introduces into his *London, a Poem, in Imitation of the Third Satire of Juvenal*, which has such sonorous cadences:

> Has Heaven reserv'd in pity to the poor
> No pathless waste, or undiscover'd shore?
> No secret island in the boundless Main?
> No peaceful desart, yet unclaim'd by Spain?

such a sudden couplet as:

> Forgive my transports on a theme like this,
> I cannot bear a French metropolis—

which, a critic has well observed, might easily have been numbered among the light verse of Mr. Hilaire Belloc, it cannot but awaken gentle mirth, not for the matter of the lines, which are not in the least risible in the original:

> *Non possum ferre, Quirites,*
> *Græcam urbem—*

but for Johnson's unexpected lapse in key, which did not impinge ludicrously on polite ears in 1738, but to our own is delicious. Again, when Wordsworth ("the Voice of God," as an admirer remarked, doubtless in an inattentive moment, "speaking through the mouth of an Englishman") begins solemnly:

> Spade! with which Wilkinson hath tilled his lands,

the effect of the "Wilkinson" even more than of the "Spade!" at once resolves the line into comedy. The dragging of the average English middle-class surname into serious verse is at all times fatal, as any poet with the least sense of the ridiculous could perceive. Elsewhere in this book will be found a funereal line of Chatterton:

> The blood-stained tomb where Smith and comfort lie,

which is clearly monumental, inspected from any position. Crabbe has an equally striking line:

> And I was ask'd and authorised to go
> To seek the firm of Clutterbuck and Co.

There is another of the same quality in Courtenay's panegyric of the Johnsonian circle:

> Harmonious JONES! who in his splendid strains
> Sings Camdeo's sports, on Agra's flowery plains,

and another, of a slightly richer texture, by Scott of Amwell:

> Methinks of friendship's frequent fate
> I hear my FROGLEY's voice complain;

and others, even more engaging, appear in certain memorial verses by the good Dr. Watts, to be read in a later page. The gulf separating such evocations from, say, Villon's

> *Berthe au grant pié, Bietris, Alys,*
> *Haremburgis qui tint le Maine . . .*

is not easy to explain immediately by pure mathematics, but one feels instinctively there is one.

So there is. Splendour of God! (as William the Conqueror would cry) there certainly is. The French blackguard marshals names like a fanfare of silver trumpets and a roll of festal drums. The English gentlemen (Mr. Courtenay a Member of Parliament, Mr. Wordsworth, *vox Dei per Anglos*, Poet Laureate and Distributor of Stamps for Cumberland and Westmorland) evoke names so marvellously prosaic that in their poetic trappings they appear rather like Garter King-of-Arms vested for a coronation in his State tabard of argent, or, azure, gules, the whole enhanced by a celluloid dickey and crowned by a small but impressive bowler hat. Could you hold in that giggle, friends? asks Horace concerning a similar phenomenon.

Bathos, as we observe, is not all. There is often found in Bad Verse that windy splurging and bombinating which makes Victor Hugo's minor rhetoric so comic and so terrible. Other plain marks are all those things connoted by poverty of the imagination, sentimentality, banality, the prosaic, the *style pompier*, and what Mr. Polly called "rockcockyo"; anæmia, obstipation, or constipation of the poetic faculty; inability to hold the key of inspiration; insufficiency of emotional content for metrical form. The function of the poet, says Sir Arthur Quiller-Couch, is to strip the Idea of triviality and the accidental and to reclothe it in beauty and concrete form. When the poet assumes the cothurnus, the chlamys, and the mask to announce that it will rain to-morrow because his corns are shooting he becomes a candidate for this book, whoever he may be. And it will be observed that with two or three exceptions all the poets represented in these pages are men and

B

women to whom Almighty God in His inscrutable providence has seen fit to deny a sense of humour. Even in the case of the exceptions their sense of humour deserts them in a crisis. The thoughtful reader may well pause here to realise how irrevocably Heaven's punishment descends from time to time on those who provoke it by Hubris. Your portentous personage invites it, and receives it. He is found everywhere ("I beg your pardon, Sir," said Douglas Jerrold, accosting a very pompous stranger in the street, "but would you mind informing me—are you anybody in particular?"), and he has produced a great deal of verse, lyric, heroic, dramatic, and pseudo-historical.

That certain delicacy on the compilers' part already mentioned forbids, again, the conjuration of eminent contemporary names, or this particular aspect of Bad Verse and some others might be discussed here with cosy intimacy and—we hope—refreshment and profit. Nevertheless one may be permitted in passing to detect the vengeance of Heaven here and there in quarters very near and dear. It was a recent Laureate who remarked of Nature:

> She sins upon a larger scale
> Because she is herself more large,

and again,

> Nothing can match, where'er we roam,
> An English wife in an English home,

and again,

> The spring-time, O the spring-time!
> Who does not know it well?
> When the little birds begin to build
> And the buds begin to swell.

It was a very great late-Victorian who wrote, perfectly seriously:

> He cancelled the ravaging plague
> With the roll of his fat off the cliff.

This, also, was written by a modern poet, greatly adored by the English People, and especially in Kensington:

> And when I clasp'd thy hand so white,
> I meant to curse thee, girl, to-night.
>
> And so I shall—Oh ! doubt not that !
> At stroke of twelve I'll curse thee twice;
> When screams the owl, when swoops the bat,
> When ghosts are out, I'll curse thee thrice.

and also this, concerning Beethoven:

> An angel by direct descent, a German by alliance,
> Thou didst intone the wonder-chords which made Despair a science.

This was written by one of the greatest of modern poets, scolding the city of Paris:

> Beautiful City, the centre and crater of European confusion,
> O you with your passionate shriek for the rights of an equal humanity,
> How often your Re-volution has proven but E-volution
> Roll'd again back on itself in the tides of a civic insanity!

also this:

> Sir, I was once a wife. I had one brief summer of bliss.
> But the Bandit had woo'd me in vain, and he stabb'd my Piero
> with this.

So we might continue a long time, letting the jewels drip slowly and reluctantly through our fingers and diving into the treasure-chest for more and more; lingering, for example, over this, by an Overseas poet of some celebrity:

> The lungs with the living gas grow light,
>   And the limbs feel the strength of ten;
> While the chest expands with its madd'ning might,
>   God's glorious oxygen.

And this, from nearer home, and probably referring
to England:

> To the land of the waiting springtime,
> To our five-meal, meat-fed men,
> To the tall deep-bosomed women,
> And the children nine and ten.

And this, engendered by a distinguished modern:
evidently in the close season:

> When will old Master Science hear the call,
> Bid us run free with life in every limb
> To breathe the poems and hear the last red rose
> Gossiping over God's grey garden-wall?

And (lastly, and regretfully enough) this, the call
of a Voice from the New World, revered alike in
Bloomsbury and Greenwich Village, N.Y.:

> With the flag.
> With the flag of sets.
> Sets of colour.
> Do you like flags.
> Blue flags smell sweetly.
> Blue flags in a whirl.
> The wind blows.
> And the automobile goes.
> Can you guess boards.
> Wood.
> Can you guess hoops.
> Barrels.
> Can you guess girls.
> Servants.
> Can you guess messages.
> In deed.

—which the judicious reader may like to compare
with recent lines of an equally modern French poet,
possibly on the same theme: [1]

> Sangsue d'encre et de cendre visse son œil dans le gâteau
> Sur les mauvais sentiments des femmes, le corset de la tempête
> Qui travaille, travaille
> Le verre dans le verre
> Et le petit animal de verre

---

[1] Tristan Tzara, *De nos Oiseaux* (Paris, 1929).

Pour le petit déjeuner de Dieu
Les yeux de cette jeune fille sont des boussoles de rébus.
Pluie de becs d'oiseau sur les yeux aux champs d'étoffe
Fermier des endroits lugubres
Un œil sur le piédestal.

"*La chûte en est jolie, amoureuse, admirable*,"
as Philinte says of the sonnet in the play. We
cite these last two poems with reservations, for we
are authoritatively informed that they are the
poetry of the future. Observe that the special
technique of the Anglo-Saxon is not constant—
there is a palpable rime in the eighth line—and
admire with us the gravity of the poet and the
solemn intensity of her preoccupation with the
little bits of bright tin and coloured glass and
wool Mother has found. We frankly admit that
we may be wrong in inserting her poem here.
Coleridge declared that not twenty lines of Scott's
verse would ever reach posterity. Time is always
making fools of the Pundits. These lines may be
on every tongue, lovingly repeated (like Euripides'
among the folk of Abdera), in 1999. *Tu autem,
Domine, miserere.*

Before concluding it may be hinted that false
patriotism is a peculiarly fruitful source of Bad
Verse; it is inevitable that this noble virtue, once
degraded, should inspire a silly kind of mouthing.
Bad patriotic verse of course existed some time
before the great nineteenth-century Nordic drive
of what H. G. Wells has called "professorial barbarity and braggart race-imperialism," with Froude
and Carlyle, Freeman and Green as its fuglemen.
At its heartiest this school produced:

> We don't want to fight,
> But, by Jingo! if we do . . .

At its most literary it has produced that lyrical and raucous contempt for lesser breeds without the Law (Latins and Celts chiefly) which leaves the shrinking reader with an impression of sawdust and belching. The general concomitants of such verse are, as G. K. Chesterton has remarked, "the eternal, complacent iteration of patriotic half-truths; the perpetual buttering over of oneself with the same stale butter; above all, the big defiances of small enemies and the very urgent challenges to very distant enemies." Such stuff was least noxious, perhaps, in the periods of the French wars, when the enemy was our own size. More recent examples are such that one might almost believe that the financiers who precede and follow the troops had written the glorifications themselves. Two not untalented precursors adorn this book, the one the Rev. Dr. Young, the celebrated author of *Night Thoughts*, and the other (to one's own astonishment) the *sympathique* Eliza Cook.

It remains to indicate the scope of this collection, which represents for the most part private addictions, and for that reason may appeal to a larger circle. It was rather a problem to fix a point of departure. Eventually we decided to begin with Cowley. Possibly the decision was unwise, for there are good things in his immediate predecessors, the alembicated Donne, the mystic Crashaw, and their school; but it was felt that their general obscurity and cragginess retard the slide into the depths. Earlier producers of Bad Verse, the Elizabethans and the Medievals, were rejected for much the same reason. When these are bad they are tiresome to a degree. Cowley is the last poet of the metaphysical school and about the first to be bad comically, and therefore makes a convenient jumping-off point. At the other end of the book is Tennyson, after whom begin those contemporaries whom politeness debars. We may point out once more that the rich mine of amateurism, especially Victorian and Edwardian, has been left practically untouched: some attractive imbecilities may have been lost thereby, but equally is it true that a fall off a cliff is more interesting than a fall off a cushion. And we sincerely trust that it is unnecessary to underline our conviction that great poets who may have graced this book are still great poets. The passing hilarities of Epiphany did not affect our fathers' adhesion to the eternal Verities.

The brief biographical notes and briefer annotations are designed to provide in as few strokes as possible a background for each poet's verse. In one case, where the most exhaustive research was unrewarded, the want has been modestly supplied by a few hypotheses, in the best manner of modern Science. For assistance in discovering and tracing many extracts to their source the compilers are greatly indebted to the enthusiasm and skill of Miss Bozman; and they particularly wish to record their gratitude to Mr. Max Beerbohm and to Messrs. Heinemann, by whose kindness they have been enabled to embellish this anthology with reproductions of eight celebrated cartoons.

They have only to add that it is their firm belief that this is on the whole a sunny, optimistic book, like J. R. Green's *Short History of the English People*, since it reveals the follies of our predecessors and proves by implication what splendid fellows we are now. This feeling has been put by an eminent modern Anglo-Saxon poet into verse which, apart from its historical and literary value and its sure technique, very admirably crystallises the Meta-physico-theologo-cosmolo-nigology to which the best modern thought, including Callisthenes, inclines, and of which a distinguished exponent was the late Dr. Pangloss. We make no apology for ending with her ringing message.

> If you glance at History's pages,
>   In all lands and eras known,
> You will find the buried ages
>   Far more wicked than our own;
> As you scan each word and letter
>   You will realise it more—
> That the world to-day is better
>   Than it ever was before.

. . . And that, in short (to echo Mr. Micawber in one of his bursts of confidence) is our own position.

D. B. W. L.

London, *January* 1930.

NOTE TO SECOND EDITION

The compilers take this opportunity of expressing their gratitude to the numbers of correspondents and reviewers who have been kind enough to assist them with criticisms, suggestions, and (best of all) indications of further specimens of Bad Verse, most of which will be found on pp. 14–23 and 224–9.

It is hoped that serious students will welcome the addition of a Subject Index.

D. B. W. L.

C. L.

London, *September* 1930.

PROEM

(*From "The Cacohymniad," Book I*)

Bad Verse I sing, and since 'twere best, I deem,
T' employ a style that suits my swelling theme,
First, in my lines some flatulence t' infuse,
I thus invoke the Muddle-headed Muse.

   Ascend, O CACOHYMNIA, *from the deep,*
Where BLACKMORE *mumbles epics in his sleep,*
While by a mud-pool endless Birthday Odes
CIBBER *recites, and charms the list'ning toads ;*
What time his placid Pegasean steed,
Browsing along th' adjacent thistly mead,
Pricks his tall ears, and lengthens out his bray
In faithful echo of his master's lay.
Adjust thy wig, eternally awry,
And wipe the gummy rheum from either eye.
Endeavour not (vain task) to tune thy lyre,
Nor stay to renovate that rusty wire ;
For in thy strain should any note be missing,
Thy sacred bird 's at hand to fill the gap with hissing.

   She comes! she comes!   Like castanets of Spain,
Clip-clop, clip-clop, her slippers strike the plain,
While from her lips proceeds th' oracular hum :
"De-dum, de-dum, de-dumty, dum de-dum."
A gander limps with outstretch'd neck before her,
And owls and jays and cuckoos hover o'er her.
Brisk at her elbow NAMBY PAMBY *skips,*
Checking her chant on quiv'ring finger-tips ;
And close behind, strutting in laurell'd state,
See! AUSTIN *arm-in-arm with* PYE *and* TATE.
Follows a crowd confus'd of wigs and hats :
HAYLEYS *and* BAYLYS, JERNINGHAMS *and* SPRATS;
A horde of DELLA CRUSCANS, *chanting, panting,*
Thrilling and shrilling, canting and re-canting ;

Bristolia's bibliopolic bard, JOE COTTLE,
Hugging three epics—and a blacking-bottle ;
T. BAKER, *who Steam's gospel best delivers ;*
The Reverend WHUR, *and Georgia's pride,* Doc. CHIVERS;
And ELLA, *who from ev'ry pore exudes*
Impassion'd transatlantic platitudes.
And who comes now, hee-hawing down the wind ?
'Tis Colley's Pegasus!   And these, entwin'd
In amorous embrace upon his crupper ?
ELIZA COOK *and* MARTIN FARQUHAR TUPPER!

   Now the cortège, advancing, nears the spot
Where rubbish from Parnassus hill is shot.
Here batter'd tropes and similes abound,
And metaphors lie mix'd in many a mound,
And oily rags of sentiment bestrew the ground.
With shouts exultant, see! th' excited troop
Rush on the spoil, and grab and grub and scoop,
And snatch and scuffle.   With indulgent mien,
Awhile the Muse surveys the busy scene ;
A tow'ring Gradus-heap she then ascends,
And, hawking thrice, the toil below suspends.
Her scholars, in a nudging, shuffling line,
Attend the utt'rance of the voice divine.
Like schoolboy's of fourteen her accents thrill,
Now rumbling deep, now stridulating shrill ;
And these her words, transcrib'd by my unworthy quill:

   "Not without dust and heat are prizes won.
Hot, dusty ones, your Muse applauds : well done!
Some words of counsel now, ere you disperse,
Your swag to file and flatten into verse.

   "Let others vie, as PINDAR *vied before,*
With eagles that monotonously soar ;
The various-gifted dabchick be your model,
Skilful to splash, and flap, and wade, and waddle,
And in that art which none achieve by thinking,
Skilfull'st of all—I mean the Art of Sinking.

   "Not that I bid you never rise at all,

Or shun th' éclat that greets a sudden fall.
So, when in yard suburban we survey
The high-stretch'd panoply of Washing-day,
Zephyrs the flutt'ring crowd inspire, uplift,
Distend the shirt, and agitate the shift ;
But should perchance th' afflatus breathe too strong, ⎫
The treach'rous prop precipitates the throng : ⎬
Let such sublime disaster oft attend your song. ⎭

"Ever you'll find me, your complaisant Muse,
Quick to inspire, whate'er the theme you choose—
Dunghills, or feather-beds, or fat-tail'd rams,
Or rum, or kilts, or eggs, or bugs, or yams.
So when some dame, in some Department Store,
Her shopping-list exhausted, orders more,
The sleek assistant, outwardly unvex'd,
Smiling exclaims, 'Thenks, moddom!   And the next ?'

"Behold the pompous funerary train
Of Enoch Arden, piscatorial swain.
'Mid tropic seas the luckless Bryan mark,
In process of bisection by a shark.
Hear ARMSTRONG *gloat on what occurs inside you*
When cook has turtle-soup'd and ven'son-pie'd you ;
And list while DYER, *in Miltonic metre,*
Recites the ailments of the fleecy bleater.
Rejoice with YOUNG *that no protective bars*
Exclude commercial blessings from the stars,
And in the Milky Way prepare to greet
A still more glorious Throgmorton Street.
Hear DARWIN, *whom no scand'lous detail ruffles,*
Record the love-lorn loneliness of truffles,
Friskings of vegetable lads and lasses,
Amours of oysters, goings-on of gases.
With fit solemnity let WORDSWORTH *tell*
How Simon's ankles swell, and swell, and swell,
And how, from Anna's couch when friends depart, ⎫
An owl, preserv'd by taxidermic art, ⎬
Can cheat the tedious time, and heal the conscious smart. ⎭

"*So sing the Masters of Bathetic Verse.*
Follow their lead : do better, doing worse.
So shall your brows be crown'd with bays unwith'ring ;
So shall the world be blither for your blith'ring ;
So——"

    Here she pauses, deep inhales the breeze,
And shakes the earth with cataclysmic sneeze.
The dust-heaps crumble, whirling clouds arise,
And all is blotted from my blinking eyes.

                    C. L.

LETCHWORTH,
  January 1930.

CONTENTS

	PAGE
PREFACE	vii
PROEM	xxi
HORS-D'ŒUVRE—I	1
HORS-D'ŒUVRE—II	14

ABRAHAM COWLEY (1618–67):
| An Archangel's Toilet . . . . . . | 25 |
| Yoicks! Gone Away! . . . . . . | 25 |

MARGARET CAVENDISH, DUCHESS OF NEWCASTLE (1624–74):
The Body: A Fancy	27
No Doubt	28
From "Nature's Dessert"	28
A Posset for Nature's Breakfast	28

JOHN DRYDEN (1631–1700):
The Return of Charles II	30
The English Fleet Goes Out	31
The Faculty at Work	32
To Account Rendered	32

JOHN BANKS (fl. 1677–96):
| The Wonder . . . . | 33 |
| Short Curse . . . . | 33 |

THOMAS SPRAT (1635–1713):
| On His Mistress Drowned . . . . . | 34 |

JOHN SHEFFIELD, DUKE OF BUCKINGHAMSHIRE (1648–1721):
| Heavy Going . . . . | 36 |
| The Blue Pencil . . . . . . | 37 |

NAHUM TATE (1652–1715):
| Ode upon the New Year . . . . . | 38 |

SIR RICHARD BLACKMORE (d. 1729):
The Chase of the Metaphor	41
From the Psalms	41
From the Book of Job	41
The Crystal Palaces	42
Possibilities	42

JOSEPH ADDISON (1672–1719):   PAGE

    Rosamond's Song 45
    King Henry's Song 46

ISAAC WATTS (1674–1748):

    Mr. Gunston is Shown round Heaven . . . 48
    A Polyglot in Paradise 48
    Mr. Mead, Mr. Bates, and Mr. Gouge . . 49
    Mrs. Warner Arrives Above 49
    On the Landing of William III . . . 49

COLLEY CIBBER (1671–1757):

    From the New Year's Ode, 1731 . . . 52
    From the Birthday Ode, 1732 53
    From Another, 1743 54

AMBROSE PHILIPS (1675–1749):

    Salute to Property 55
    Ode to Miss Margaret Pulteney . . . 56
    To the Right Hon. Robert Walpole, Esq. . . 56

JOHN, LORD HERVEY (1696–1743):

    Nature Queries 58

JOHN ARMSTRONG (1709–79):

    Rustic Interior 61
    Advice to the Stout 61
    The Gastric Muse 62
    On Washing 62
    On Feather Beds 63

EDWARD YOUNG (1683–1765):

    A Submarine Jaunt 65
    Seascape 65
    A Runcible Thought 66
    "Sting Her Up!" 66
    From the "Ode to the King" 67
    From "Ocean, an Ode" 69
    To a Solemn Musick 72
    Final Pæan 72
    Ye Nations, Tremble! Parliament has Met . 73
    With a Yo, Ho, Ho 74
    La Pudeur Française 75

JOHN DYER (1700–58):

    Pastoral 76
    The Insensible Hottentot 77
    The House Beautiful 78
    Leeds for Pleasure 78

CONTENTS

WILLIAM SHENSTONE (1714–63):   PAGE
    Home Industries First 80
    Goats and Botanists 82
    The Chase of Jessy 82

JOSEPH WARTON (1722–1800):
    Le Spleen 85

JAMES GRAINGER (1721–67):
    Bryan and Pereene 88
    Crescendo 90
    The Shame of France 90
    Advice to Slave-Owners 90
    Call to the Muse 91

THOMAS WARTON, THE YOUNGER (1728–90):
    Of George, and Property 92

EDWARD JERNINGHAM (1727–1812):
    Il Latte 95

CHRISTOPHER SMART (1722–71):
    Hops and Props 97
    The Nail in the Grass 98

OLIVER GOLDSMITH (1728–74):
    Entry of the Villagers 99
    Cause and Effect 100
    A Sombre Moment. 100

JOHN DUNCOMBE (1729–86):
    Females, Sacred and Profane 102

ERASMUS DARWIN (1731–1802):
    Eliza at the Battle. 106
    Fine Figure of a Nymph. 107
    "Ae Fond Kiss, and Then——" . . . 108
    The Maiden Truffle 108
    The Birth of KNO_3 108

THOMAS CHATTERTON (1752–70):
    Mr. Baker is Well 109
    Miss Hoyland is Coy 110
    Mr. Smith is Dead 110

GEORGE CRABBE (1754–1832):
    A Business Man's Lair 111
    The Baileys 112
    A Bright Morning 113
    Invitation to the Waltz 113

ROBERT BURNS (1759–96):   PAGE
     Verses on the Death of Sir James Hunter Blair.   .   114

ROBERT MERRY ("DELLA CRUSCA") (1755–98):
     Elegy Written after reading the "Sorrows of Werter"   117
     The Rush to the Lakes   118
     Some Terrify Lions   118
     The Poet is Piqued   119
     The Tiff   119

HANNAH COWLEY ("ANNA MATILDA") (1743–1809):
     Off Duty   122
     The Well-Aimed Tear   122

DELLA CRUSCANS (*fl.* 1785–92):
     Moods   124
     Notice to Tourists   125

MARY ROBINSON ("PERDITA") (1758–1800):
     The Temple of Chastity   127
     The Vest of Myrtle   127

JOSEPH COTTLE (1770–1853):
     Virtue Protests   129
     Ratiocinative   130
     The Affectionate Heart   130

ROBERT SOUTHEY (1774–1843):
     George III Enters Paradise   131

JAMES HENRY LEIGH HUNT (1784–1859):
     Lovers' Exchange   133
     Domestic Chat   133
     "What with This and That——"   .   .   .   134
     Aphrodite Adiposa   135

HENRY KIRKE WHITE (1785–1806):
     The Evening Stroll   136
     The Evening Sin   137
     Britannia Rejecta   137

GEORGE GORDON, LORD BYRON (1788–1824):
     The Tear   139
     The Prisoner Scolds   140
     Cæsar Sings   141

CONTENTS

WILLIAM WORDSWORTH (1770–1850):   PAGE
Odd Case of Mr. Gill 144
(Oxford Street?) 144
The Aged, Aged Man 145
Asked and Answered 145
The Old Huntsman 145
The Poet Reveals All 147
Baffled 149
The Course Prescribed 149
A Mother's Quest 150
Insensibility 150
The Stuffed Owl 150
Decadence; or, The Umbrella 151
A Worm's Life Not Everything 151
An Experiment that Failed 152

JOHN KEATS (1795–1821):
To Some Ladies 153

CORNELIUS WHUR (1782–1853):
The Female Friend 156
The First-Rate Wife 157
The Unfortunate Gentleman 158
From "The Rose-Covered Grave" . . . 159
Catastrophe 160
The Poet Questions the Ant 161
And So Home 161

ROBERT POLLOK (1798–1827):
A Contretemps 162
Proximities 163
The Once-Over 163

RALPH WALDO EMERSON (1803–82):
Get-Together Song 164
Efficiency 165

THOMAS HAYNES BAYLY (1797–1839):
Oh, No! We Never Mention Her . . . 167
Something to Love 168
I'm Saddest When I Sing 168
The Soldier's Tear 169
I'd be a Butterfly 169

ELIZABETH OAKES SMITH (1806–93):
Insect Affection 171

ROBERT MONTGOMERY (1807–55):
Marine Vignette 174
A Request 174
Fore and Aft 175
On the Revolution 176

CHARLES MACKAY (1814–89):   PAGE
    The Earl and the Girl 177
    A Challenge 179
    Only a Thought 179

EDGAR ALLAN POE (1809–49):
    Prone 180
    Bridal Ballad 181
    Eulalie 182

THOMAS HOLLEY CHIVERS (*fl.* 1840):
    Miss Adair 183
    Miss Lee 184
    A Call 185
    From "The Vigil of Aiden" 185

ELIZABETH BARRETT BROWNING (1809–61):
    Snoblesse Oblige 187

HENRY WADSWORTH LONGFELLOW (1807–82):
    Excelsior 190

T. BAKER (*fl.* 1837–57):
    Lord Stanhope's Steamer 193
    On the Cork Packet, 1837 194
    Great Western Days 194
    The Death of Huskisson 195
    Roses All the Way 195
    The Railway Boom, 1845 196
    A Lesson for the Proud 197
    Vision of the World, regenerated by the Gospel and the
      Power of Steam 197

ELIZA COOK (1818–89):
    Trombone Solo 200
    Live and Let Live 201
    Becalmed in the Tropics 201
    A Thought 202
    From "The Old Arm-Chair" 202
    Entry of the Marines 202
    A Thought 203

SAMUEL CARTER (*fl.* 1848–51):
    Incident in Italy 204
    The Passing of Arthur 206
    Pæan 207

MARTIN FARQUHAR TUPPER (1810–89):
    Portrait of a Victorian Author . . . 209
    The Marriage Market 210
    The Poor Relation; or, Pious Hope Frustrated . 212
    The Art of Giving (1850) 213

CONTENTS

JOHN CLOSE (1816–91):   PAGE

    The Beelah Viaduct 215
    Haloes, Not Hats 216
    Mentem Mortalia Tangunt 216

SYDNEY THOMPSON DOBELL (1824–74):
    A Timely Hint 217

EDWARD ROBERT BULWER LYTTON, EARL OF LYTTON
    ("OWEN MEREDITH") (1831–91):
    Check to Song 219
    Financial Note 220
    The Count and the Lady 221
    Sordid Scene 222

GEORGE EVELEIGH (fl. 1863):
    A Divine Mission 224

EDWARD EDWIN FOOT (fl. 1867):
    Disaster at Sea 226
    A State Occasion 227
    The Good Young Squire 228
    A Graceful Divine 228
    A Lisp in Numbers 229

ADAM LINDSAY GORDON (1833–70):
    From "Ashtaroth," a Drama 230
    The Fight in the Cave 232
    A Warning 232

JULIA MOORE (1847–1920):
    Steam: The Seamy Side 234
    Byron: A Critical Survey 235
    A Noble Structure 237
    Hic Finis Rapto 238
    The Poet is Scornful 240
    A Call (1876) 240
    Anti-Bacchics 241

ALFRED, LORD TENNYSON (1809–92):
    Ode Sung at the Opening of the International Exhibi-
      tion 242
    The Lord of Burleigh 244
    Ocean-Spoil Alive, O! 247
    Riflemen Form 247
    Iphigenia in Extremis 248

POSTPRANDIAL 249

SUBJECT INDEX 253

INDEX OF AUTHORS 263

ILLUSTRATIONS

STATESMAN OF OLDEN TIME, MAKING WITHOUT WISH FOR
EMOLUMENT A FLAT BUT FAITHFUL VERSION OF THE
GEORGICS, IN ENGLISH HEXAMETERS . *Frontispiece*

OMAR KHAYYAM . . . . . *facing page* 42

ROBERT BROWNING, TAKING TEA WITH THE
BROWNING SOCIETY . . . . ,, 76

MR. MATTHEW ARNOLD . . . . ,, 108

WILLIAM WORDSWORTH, IN THE LAKE DISTRICT,
AT CROSS-PURPOSES . . . . ,, 148

WALT WHITMAN, INCITING THE BIRD OF
FREEDOM TO SOAR . . . . ,, 172

MR. TENNYSON, READING "IN MEMORIAM"
TO HIS SOVEREIGN . . . . ,, 242

THE MINOR POET AND HIS MUSE . . *Endpaper*

*Printed in this book with the kind permission of Sir Max Beerbohm
and Messrs. William Heinemann Ltd.*

HORS-D'ŒUVRE

I

I shall go down to Bedfordshire to-morrow.
ALEXANDER SMITH, A LIFE-DRAMA.

Spade! with which Wilkinson hath tilled his lands.
WORDSWORTH, TO THE SPADE OF A FRIEND

Inoculation, heavenly maid, descend! [1]
ANON.

Hope kicks the curl'd heads of conspiring stars.
CRASHAW, HOPE.

How brave a prospect is a bright backside! [2]
HENRY VAUGHAN.

Rennie's conoidal triple-bladed screw.
T. BAKER, THE STEAM ENGINE.

Not without virtues was the prince.   Who is?
LEIGH HUNT, THE STORY OF RIMINI.

A garden is a lovesome thing, God wot! [3]
T. E. BROWN, MY GARDEN.

[1] Opening of an Oxford copy of verses on the two Suttons, quoted by Coleridge in *Biographia Literaria*.
[2] This was too much for the Rev. H. F. Lyte, who in his edition of Vaughan amended the two last words to "traversed plain."
[3] From the *Oxford Book of English Verse*.

O Dawson, monarch of my heart!
SHENSTONE, JEMMY DAWSON.

Sadly they charm'd, and dismally they pleas'd.[1]
STEELE, THE PROCESSION.

He suddenly dropt dead of heart-disease.
TENNYSON, SEA-DREAMS.

But life is oft so like a dream, we know not where we are
MARTIN TUPPER, THE DREAM OF AMBITION.

Her smile was silent as the smile on corpses three hours
old.
EARL OF LYTTON, LOVE AND SLEEP.

He fell upon his hands in warm wet slop.
ALFRED AUSTIN, THE HUMAN TRAGEDY.

Irks care the crop-full bird? Frets doubt the maw-
crammed beast?
BROWNING RABBI BEN EZRA.

His hands were changed to feet, and he in short
Became a stag.
UNIVERSITY POET UNKNOWN, ACTÆON.

Some of the skilful teach, and some deny
That yams improve the soil.
GRAINGER, THE SUGAR-CANE.

[1] Of the maids of honour in mourning for Queen Mary.

Our Euripides, the human,
  With his droppings of warm tears.
          MRS. BROWNING, WINE OF CYPRUS.

Under the Tropic is our language spoke,
And part of Flanders hath receiv'd our yoke.
              WALLER, UPON THE
          DEATH OF THE LORD PROTECTOR.

      Bird of the wilderness,
      Blithesome and cumberless.[1]
          JAMES HOGG, TO A SKYLARK.

And thou, Dalhousie, the great God of War,
Lieutenant-Colonel to the Earl of Mar.
                        ANON.

    God in the wilderness his table spread,
    And in his airy ovens bak'd their bread.
          BLACKMORE, SONG OF MOSES.

  Then I fling the fisherman's flaccid corpse
  At the feet of the fisherman's wife.
          ALFRED AUSTIN, THE WIND.

  Grave Jonas Kindred, Sybil Kindred's sire,
  Was six feet high, and look'd six inches higher.
          CRABBE, THE FRANK COURTSHIP.

---

[1] "A couplet which, I believe, had it occurred in a work by
a Babu, would have been treated as a rich example of comic
English."—J. C. SQUIRE.

Forgive my transports on a theme like this,
I cannot bear a French metropolis.
JOHNSON, LONDON.

The management of tyros of eighteen
Is difficult, their punishment obscene.
COWPER, TIROCINIUM.

Her airy guard prepares the softest down
From Peace's wing to line the nuptial crown.[1]
WILLIAM HAYLEY.

Sweet Roses may over a sepulchre creep,
Whilst what it contains makes the Moralist weep.
ELIZABETH TURNER, OUTSIDE AND INSIDE.

So 'tis with Christians, Nature being weak,
While in this world, are liable to leak.
WILLIAM BALMFORD, THE SEAMAN'S
SPIRITUAL COMPANION.

The homebound rustic counts his wage,
The same last week, the same the next.
ALFRED AUSTIN, THE VILLAGE CHURCH.

Earth from afar has heard Thy fame,
And worms have learnt to lisp Thy name.
HYMNODIST UNKNOWN.

[1] "The image of a guardian angel holding Peace with the firmness of an Irish housewife, and plucking her steadily in order to line a nuptial crown (which must have been a sort of sunbonnet) with the down thereof, will probably be admitted to be not easily surpassable."—SAINTSBURY.

Only he felt he could no more dissemble,
And kiss'd her, mouth to mouth, all of a tremble.[1]
LEIGH HUNT, THE STORY OF RIMINI.

Since Brunswick's smile has authorised my Muse,[2]
Chaste be her conduct, and sublime her views.
YOUNG, THE INSTALMENT.

No more will I endure Love's pleasing pain,
Nor round my heart's leg tie his galling chain.[3]
A YOUNG TRADESMAN POET.

Backward the sun, an unknown motion, went;
The stars gazed on, and wondered what he meant.
COWLEY, DAVIDEIS.

Tell me what viands, land or streams produce,
The large, black, female, moulting crab excel?
GRAINGER, THE SUGAR-CANE.

Now Vengeance has a brood of eggs,
But Patience must be hen.
GEORGE MEREDITH,
ARCHDUCHESS ANNE.

How the warm planet ripens and sublimes
The well-bak'd beauties of the southern climes!
DRYDEN, DON SEBASTIAN.

---

[1] Intended to represent Dante's "*La bocca mi baciò tutto tremante.*"

[2] With a pension of two hundred pounds.

[3] Quoted by Coleridge in *Biographia Literaria.*

O Sire of Song! Sonata-King! Sublime and loving Master,
The sweetest soul that ever struck an octave in disaster!
ERIC MACKAY, BEETHOVEN.

She [1] tried her heavy foot from ground to rear,
And rais'd the heel, but the toe's rooted there.
COWLEY, DAVIDEIS.

Poor South!   Her books get fewer and fewer,
She was never much given to literature.
J. GORDON COOGLER.

When with staid mothers' milk and sunshine warmed
The pasture's frisky innocents bucked up.
ALFRED AUSTIN,
THE HUMAN TRAGEDY.

The ardent tourist who gay scenes admires
To join his train with rapt'rous joy aspires.
T. BAKER, THE STEAM ENGINE.

Come, saints, and drop a tear or two
On the dear bosom of your God.
DR. WATTS.

For that which makes our lives delightful prove
Is a genteel sufficiency and love.
JOHN POMFRET,
TO A FRIEND INCLINED TO MARRY.

[1] Lot's wife.

Love, though an egotist, can deify
A vulgar fault, and drape the gross with grace.
ALFRED AUSTIN,
THE HUMAN TRAGEDY.

The soul, aspiring, pants its source to mount,
As streams meander level with their fount.[1]
ROBERT MONTGOMERY,
THE OMNIPRESENCE OF THE DEITY.

I'd freely rove through Tempe's vale, or scale the giant
    Alp,
Where roses list the bulbul's tale, or snow-wreaths crown
    the scalp.
ELIZA COOK, ENGLAND.

Apollo. Draughts dregward loose tongue tie.
Lachesis.   I'd see, did no web
  Set eyes somehow winking.
Apollo.   Drains-deep lies their purge.
BROWNING,
PARLEYINGS WITH CERTAIN PEOPLE.

Leonora.   I look on chearfulness
  As on the health of virtue.
Alonzo.   Virtue!—Damn——!
YOUNG, THE REVENGE.

In Rome too liberty once reign'd, in Rome
The female virtues were allow'd to bloom,
And bloom they did.
THOMAS SEWARD,
ON THE FEMALE RIGHT TO LITERATURE.

[1] "On the whole, the worst similitude in the world."—
MACAULAY.

Knee-deep in fern stand startled doe and fawn,
And lo! there gleams upon a spacious lawn
An Earl's marine retreat.
ALEXANDER SMITH,
SQUIRE MAURICE.

But say, ye boon-companions, in what strains,
What grateful strains, shall I record the praise
Of their best produce, heart-recruiting rum?
GRAINGER, THE SUGAR-CANE.

So past the strong heroic soul away.
And when they buried him, the little port
Had seldom seen a costlier funeral.
TENNYSON, ENOCH ARDEN.

Weeping o'er thy sacred urn,
Ever shall the Muses mourn;
Sadly shall their numbers flow,
Ever elegant in woe.
AMBROSE PHILIPS,
TO THE MEMORY OF LORD HALIFAX.

O may thy powerful word
    Inspire the feeble worm
To rush into thy kingdom, Lord,
    And take it as by storm.
THE WESLEYAN HYMN BOOK.

When the plain truth Tradition seem'd to know,
And simply pointed to the harmless cow,
Doubt and distrust to reason might appeal,
But, when hope triumph'd, what did Jenner feel?
ROBERT BLOOMFIELD,
GOOD NEWS FROM THE FARM.

Hail, mighty Monarch! whom desert alone
Would, without birthright, raise up to the throne;
Thy virtues shine particularly nice,
Ungloomed with a confinity to vice.

LAURENCE EUSDEN,
POET LAUREATE, TO GEORGE II.

Since 'tis my doom, love's undershrieve,
    Why this reprieve?
Why doth my she-advowson fly
    Incumbency?

JOHN CLEVELAND, TO JULIA.

When savage War, disarm'd, exhausted, stood
Aghast in Superstition's ebbing flood,
Astonish'd Earth the Bible saw remain,
The deathless champion of the reeking plain.

THOMAS HOGG, THE BIBLE.

His cheek was worn; his back bent double
    Beneath the iron box he bore;
And in his walk there seem'd such trouble
    You saw his feet were sore.

EARL OF LYTTON, THE PEDLAR.

Europe now of bleeding wounds
Sadly shall no more complain;
GEORGE the jars of jealous crowns
Heals with halcyon days again.

COLLEY CIBBER, BIRTHDAY ODE.

To REYNOLDS, Muse, that mass of beauty, rise;
Her mien how charming, and how bright her eyes!
Can SMITH unnoted pass, so fram'd for praise?
Ev'n Britain's Court grows brighter with her rays!

ANON., c. 1709,
To THE CELEBRATED BEAUTIES OF THE COURT.

Her shining look exalts the gazing swain,
But oh! within he feels consuming pain.
So sparkling flames raise water to a smile,
Yet the pleas'd liquor pines, and lessens all the while.

IBID.

O never, never she'll forget
    The happy, happy day
When in the church, before God's priest,
    She gave herself away.

AUTHOR UNKNOWN

And now, kind friends, what I have wrote,
    I hope you will pass o'er,
And not criticise as some have done
    Hitherto herebefore.

JULIA MOORE,
THE SWEET SINGER OF MICHIGAN.

Napoleon hoped that all the world would fall beneath his
    sway;
He failed in this ambition; and where is he to-day?
Neither the nations of the East nor the nations of the
    West
Have thought the thing Napoleon thought was to their
    interest.

A LIEUTENANT-COLONEL POET.

Dash back that ocean with a pier,
  Strow yonder mountain flat,
A railway there, a tunnel here,
  Mix me this Zone with that!
                TENNYSON, MECHANOPHILUS.

Hark! she bids all her friends adieu;
Some angel calls her to the spheres;
Our eyes the radiant saint pursue
Through liquid telescopes of tears.
          DR. WATTS, ON THE SUDDEN DEATH
               OF MRS. MARY PEACOCK.

Entrapt inside a submarine,
With death approaching on the scene,
The crew compose their minds to dice,
More for the pleasure than the vice.
     CONGRESSMAN H. C. CANFIELD, ELEGY ON THE
          LOSS OF U.S. SUBMARINE S4.

Thought cannot comprehend, or words express,
Nor can they possibly, while I survive, be less.
   Good Heav'n had been extremely kind
If it had struck me dead, or struck me blind.
               JOHN POMFRET,
        ELEAZAR'S LAMENT OVER JERUSALEM.

In ancient days ere Britons ruled our Ind,
No man but mocked at Life, at Honour grinned,
But now benignant British banners have swiftly brought
Security of life and pelf and freedom of Thought.
                              A BABU POET.

Too much in man's imperfect state
  Mistake produces useless pain.
Methinks, of Friendship's frequent fate
  I hear my FROGLEY's voice complain.

JOHN SCOTT OF AMWELL.

O Moon, when I gaze on thy beautiful face,
Careering along through the boundaries of space,
The thought has often come into my mind
If I ever shall see thy glorious behind.

A HOUSEMAID POET.[1]

Against the haloed lattice-panes
The bridesmaid sunned her breast;
Then to the glass turned tall and free,
And braced and shifted daintily
Her loin-belt through her cote-hardie.

D. G. ROSSETTI, THE BRIDE'S PRELUDE.

    The work is done!
    The distant Sun
His smile supplies! exalts my voice!
    Through Earth's wide bound
    Shall GEORGE resound,
My theme, my duty, and my choice.

YOUNG, ODE TO THE KING.

[1] Quoted by Robert Ross in the *Academy*.

Whene'er along the ivory disks are seen
The rapid traces of the dark gangrene,
When caries comes, with stealthy pace, to throw
Corrosive ink-spots on those banks of snow,
Brook no delay, ye trembling, suffering Fair,
But fly for refuge to the Dentist's care.

SOLYMAN BROWN, THE DENTIAD.

Mysterious Magnet! ere thy use was known,
Fear clad the deep in horrors not its own;
But when thy trembling point vouchsafed to guide,
Astonish'd nations rush'd into the tide,
While o'er the rocky wave and billowy wild
Young Commerce plumed his eagle-wing, and smiled.

GEORGE WADDINGTON, COLUMBUS (CAMBRIDGE
PRIZE POEM, 1813).

So it is not the speech which tells, but the impulse which
    goes with the saying,
And it is not the words of the prayer, but the yearning
    back of the praying. . . .
And therefore I say again, though I am Art's own true
    lover,
That it is not Art, but Heart, which wins the wide world
    over.

ELLA WHEELER WILCOX.

D

II

Thou little bounder,[1] rest.
JOHN RUSKIN.

With a goad he punched each furious dame.
CHAPMAN, TRANSLATION OF THE ILIAD.

Salubrious hinds the festive dance explore.
JOHN NICHOLS, SPRING.

Hail, honour'd Wickliff, enterprising sage!
SHENSTONE, THE RUINED ABBEY.

His arrows chink as often as he [2] jogs.
HOBBES, TRANSLATION OF THE ILIAD.

A fly that up and down himself doth shove.
WORDSWORTH, TO SLEEP.

Tho' something like moisture conglobes in my eye.
BURNS, ADDRESS TO WILLIAM TYTLER.

Through the long noon coo, crooning through the coo.
GEORGE MEREDITH, LOVE IN THE VALLEY.

I have no pain, dear mother, now; but oh, I am so dry!
EDWARD FARMER, LITTLE JIM.

[1] Addressing his heart.
[2] Apollo, coming down to destroy the Greeks. See Iliad i, 46.

Will you oftly
Murmur softly?
　　　　　Mrs. Browning.

So long he seems to stop
On thy bald awful head, O sovran Blanc.
　　　　Coleridge, Hymn before Sunrise.

Like as the hart doth pant and bray
The well-spring to attain.
　　　　Sternhold and Hopkins, Psalm XLII.

He ceased his vows, and, with disdainful air,
He turn'd to blast the late exultant fair.
　　　　Shenstone, The Judgment of Hercules.

Such was the sob and the mutual throb
Of the knight embracing Jane.
　　　　Thomas Campbell, Ritter Ban.

The beetle booms adown the glooms
And bumps along the clumps.
　　　　Author Unknown.

The two divinest things that man has got,
A lovely woman in a rural spot.[1]
　　　　Leigh Hunt.

King Edward the Sev'nth, son of noble reigns,
Husband of one of the Ancient Danes.
　　　　Author Unknown.

[1] Parodied thus by Patmore:

"The two divinest things this world can grab,
A handsome woman in a hansom cab."

Where loud the blackbird cheers his bride
By some umbrageous vicarage.

ALFRED AUSTIN.

Why streams the life-blood from that female throat?
She sprinkled gravy on a guest's new coat.

AMERICAN ANTI-SLAVERY POET UNKNOWN.

Scarcely had she [1] begun to wash,
When she was aware of the grisly gash.

WILLIAM MAGINN, HOMERIC BALLADS.

I might comply—but how will Bloomer act,
When he becomes acquainted with the fact?

CRABBE.

Reach me a Handcerchiff, Another yet,
And yet another, for the last is wett.

ANON., A FUNERAL ELEGIE UPON THE
DEATH OF GEORGE SONDS, ESQ., 1658.

These vales were saddened by a common gloom,
When good Jemima perished in her bloom.

WORDSWORTH, EPITAPH ON MRS. QUILLINAN.

And when upon your dainty breast I lay
My wearied head, more soft than eiderdown.

WILLIAM NATHAN STEDMAN.

The game is ancient, manly, and employs,
In its departments, women, men, and boys.

CARNEGIE OF PITARROW, THE GOLFIAD.

[1] Eurycleia, bathing the feet of Ulysses.

But Heav'n of you [1] took such Peculiar Care
That soon the Royal Breach it did repair.

THOMAS SHADWELL.

This piteous news so much it shocked her,
She quite forgot to send the Doctor.

WORDSWORTH, THE IDIOT BOY.

Who weeps for strangers? Mary wept
For George and Sarah Green.

WORDSWORTH, GEORGE AND SARAH GREEN.

Dust to dust, and ashes to ashes,
Into the tomb the Great Queen dashes.

A BABU POET, ON THE DEATH OF
QUEEN VICTORIA.

My heart is in the grave with her—
The family went abroad.

ALEXANDER SMITH.

Across the wires the gloomy message came:
"He is not better; he is much the same."

UNIVERSITY POET UNKNOWN, ON THE
RECOVERY OF THE PRINCE OF WALES.

Once more the Ass, with motion dull,
Upon the pivot of his skull
Turned round his long left ear.

WORDSWORTH, PETER BELL.

[1] William III, wounded at the Battle of the Boyne.

The clock stands at the noon;
I am weary, I have sewn,
Sweet, for thee, a wedding-gown.

MRS. BROWNING.

Saliva, chyle, bile,
Pancreatic juice, serum, and phlegm,
There Adam lay supine—a well-shaped man.

WILLIAM BOYCE,
MAN'S FIRST ESTATE ON EARTH.

Then the maiden Aunt
Took this fair day for text, and from it preach'd
An universal culture for the crowd.

TENNYSON, THE PRINCESS.

Ah, lovely appearance of death!
What sight upon earth is so fair?
Not all the gay pageants that breathe
Can with a dead body compare.

CHARLES WESLEY,
ON THE SIGHT OF A CORPSE.

O silent tickler of the human brain!—
The infant's, boyhood's, manhood's, and old age'—
In some thou bidest with consoling strain;
In others, burning with revengeful rage.

EDWARD EDWIN FOOT, THOUGHT.

Oh, sad the wreaths to the Royal one,
King Edward, Queen Victoria's son;
Yet still they go in great profusion,
The death of him is no illusion.

AUTHOR UNKNOWN.

The oars of Ithaca dip so
  Softly into the sea,
They waken not Calypso,
  And the hero wanders free.

MORTIMER COLLINS.

. . . My grave's a bed,
  Where I lie down on roses;
I lie in state, and meditate
  Upon the law of Moses.

HYMNODIST UNKNOWN.

The frog he sits upon the bank
  And catches bugs and flies,
And after he gets tired of that
  He just jumps in and dives.

JAMES K. ELMORE, OF ALAMO, IND.

A wreath of orange-blossoms,
  When next we met, she wore.
The expression of her features
  Was more thoughtful than before.

HAYNES BAYLY,
SHE WORE A WREATH OF ROSES.

So Samson, when his hair was lost,
Met the Philistines to his cost,
Shook his huge limbs with vain surprise,
Made feeble flight, and lost his eyes.

HYMNODIST UNKNOWN.

The bed-ridden man sprang up, and cried,
And reached the door, but there he died;
And his sickly daughter, with frenzied pains,
Dragged from the fire his old remains.

WILLIAM HOWITT, THE WIND IN A RAGE.

Oysters, most excellent food since flesh became
An article of use for man's estate;
And ever since the Fall you'll find these fish
In season every month containing "R."

WILLIAM BOYCE,
MAN'S FIRST ESTATE ON EARTH.

The Eternal heard, and from the heavenly quire
Chose out the Cherub with the flaming sword,
And bad him swiftly drive the approaching fire
From where our naval magazines were stored.

DRYDEN, ANNUS MIRABILIS.

By whom shall Jacob now arise?
For Jacob's friends are few;
And what may fill us with surprise,
They seem divided too.

HYMNODIST UNKNOWN.

And if these merits hardly make amends
For gaps confessed, add a most noble gait
And blameless life, he was, 't must be allowed,
A man of whom might any girl be proud.

ALFRED AUSTIN, THE HUMAN TRAGEDY.

O the fathomless love that has deigned to approve
  And prosper the work of my hands!
With my pastoral crook I went over the brook,
  And behold, I am spread into bands.

CHARLES WESLEY, BIRTHDAY HYMN.

By all the ancient gods of Rome and Greece,
I love my daughter better than my niece.
If any one should ask the reason why,
I'd tell them—"Nature makes the stronger tie."

OLD DRAMATIST.[1]

Her lips, they are redder than coral
  That under the ocean grows;
She is sweet, she is fair, she is moral,
  My beautiful Georgian rose!

AUTHOR UNKNOWN.

Ah!—see that shade which glides along my room,
  Steals by my sight in slow-stepp'd solemn pace,
Clad from the clayey wardrobe of a tomb,
  In trailing robes that cover half the place!

MR. T., NIGHT.[2]

With these are many more convened;
  They know not I have been so far;—
I see them there, in number nine,
  Beneath the spreading Weymouth-pine!
I see them—there they are!

WORDSWORTH, PETER BELL.

---

[1] Quoted in *Curiosities of Literature.*

[2] From Bell's *Classical Arrangement of Fugitive Poetry,* viii, 61.

There we leave her,[1]
There we leave her,
Far from where her swarthy kindred roam,
In the Scarlet Fever,
Scarlet Fever,
Scarlet Fever Convalescent Home.

AUTHOR UNKNOWN.

I saw the tears start in her eye,
And trickle down her cheek;
Like falling stars across the sky
Escaping from their Maker's eye:
I saw, but spared to speak.

PHILIP JAMES BAILEY, FESTUS.

With heart compact as truth the cabbage stands,
With trickling gems bedropt in twinkling play;
There nodding onions rang'd like marshall'd bands.
The sluggard carrot sleeps his days in bed;
The crippled pea alone that cannot stand;
With vegetable marrow, rich and grand.

JOHN BIDLAKE, THE COUNTRY PARSON.

A bad act lives for ever,
A good one never dies,
But with this difference—
The one causes a beautiful sensation
To pass through the system
That makes this Earth a Heaven—
The other Hades.

EVAN LLEWELLYN, GIDDY MARY, AND
OTHER POEMS AND SONGS, 1843.

[1] An invalid gipsy.

I always knew what sort of weather
  We were going to have,
For Cynthia never wore her feather
  When the weather would be bad.

But when the days were warm and bright
  Cynthia wore a feather,
Sometimes black and sometimes white,
  The colour doesn't count whatever.

AUTHOR UNKNOWN.

ABRAHAM COWLEY (1618–67)

"Oh Gad!" says the lovely Belinda in *The Old Bachelor*, "I have a great passion for Cowley—don't you admire him?" "Oh, madam," says Sharper, "he was our English Horace." This was in 1693, when the poetry of ABRAHAM COWLEY was already more raved of than read. Still he had had during his lifetime the consolation of being the accepted authority, with his *Pindarique Odes* and others, on cultivated English verse. His first collection was published at seventeen; at twenty-two his Latin comedy *Naufragium Joculare* was played by the gentlemen of Trinity, Cambridge. He joined his friend Crashaw at Oxford later, having taken sides with the Court, whom he followed into exile in France. In 1656 he came over to London on a secret mission, was thrown into prison, and was released on a bail of a thousand pounds which hung over him till the Restoration; which event did not bring him anticipated rewards, in spite of an *Ode on the Blessed Restoration*. He lived comfortably enough notwithstanding, enjoyed the incense of his contemporaries, and died (according to Pope) of the consequences of spending a July night under a hedge on the return, with his genial clergyman friend Sprat, later Bishop of Rochester, from a "repast of *Attick* Tast," with wine.

Cowley's bad verse has plenty of the extravagances of the metaphysical school. The picture of the Archangel of the Annunciation choosing the new season's suitings in a celestial Savile Row is pleasing enough. The second extract is more broadly comic, and we perceive Dr. Harvey, discoverer of the circulation of the blood, chasing Nature, that coy and aged spinster, across country with all the relentless gusto of a Jorrocks ("Leather breeches Mr. Ratcliffe spoke kindly of") and finally whooping her down:

> "but ere she was aware,
> Harvey was with her there."

The exquisitely prosaic image of the concluding lines is also noteworthy.

An Archangel's Toilet

WHEN Gabriel (no bless'd spirit more kind or fair)
Bodies and clothes himself with thick'ned air;
All like a comely youth in life's fresh bloom,
Rare workmanship, and wrought by heavenly loom!
He took for skin a cloud most soft and bright
That e'er the mid-day sun pierced through with light;
Upon his cheeks a lively blush he spread,
Washed from the morning beauty's deepest red;
A harmless flaming meteor shone for hair,
And fell adown his shoulders with loose care:
He cuts out a silk mantle from the skies,
Where the most sprightly azure pleas'd the eyes;
This he with starry vapours spangles all,
Took in their prime ere they grow ripe and fall;
Of a new rainbow, ere it fret or fade,
The choicest piece took out, a scarf is made;
Small streaming clouds he does for wings display,
Not virtuous lovers' sighs more soft than they;
These he gilds o'er with the sun's richest rays,
Caught gliding o'er pure streams on which he plays.
Thus drest, the joyful Gabriel posts away,
And carries with him his own glorious day.

DAVIDEIS, BK. II.

Yoicks! Gone Away!

COY Nature (which remain'd, though aged grown,
A beauteous virgin still, enjoy'd by none,
    Nor seen unveil'd by any one),
When Harvey's violent passion she did see,
    Began to tremble and to flee,
Took sanctuary, like Daphne, in a tree:
There Daphne's lover stopt, and thought it much
    The very leaves of her to touch,
But Harvey, our Apollo, stopt not so,

Into the bark and root he after her did go. . . .
What should she do? through all the moving wood
Of lives endow'd with sense she took her flight;
Harvey pursues, and keeps her still in sight.
But as the deer long-hunted takes a flood,
She leapt at last into the winding streams of blood;
Of man's Meander all the purple reaches made,
 Till at the heart she stay'd,
 Where, turning head, and at a bay,
Thus, by well-purgèd ears, was she o'erheard to say:
"Here sure shall I be safe," said she;
"None will be able sure to see
 This my retreat, but only He
 Who made both it and me.
The heart of man, what art can e'er reveal?
 A wall impervious between
 Divides the very parts within,
And doth the heart of man ev'n from itself conceal."
 She spoke, but ere she was aware,
 Harvey was with her there. . . .

 Before the liver understood
 The noble scarlet dye of blood,
 Before one drop was by it made,
Or brought into it, to set up the trade;
 Before the untaught heart began to beat
The tuneful march to vital heat,
From all the souls that living buildings rear,
Whether implied for earth, or sea, or air,
Whether it in the womb or egg be wrought,
A strict account to him is hourly brought,
 How the great fabric does proceed,
What time and what materials it does need.
He so exactly does the work survey
As if he hir'd the workers by the day.

ODE UPON DR. HARVEY.

MARGARET CAVENDISH, DUCHESS OF
NEWCASTLE (1624–74)

LAMB's beloved "thrice-noble Margaret Newcastle" and Horace Walpole's "fertile pedant" met William Cavendish in Paris in 1645, during the Civil War, while she was maid of honour to Queen Henrietta Maria, and married him in the same year; after which she divided her efforts for some time between endeavouring to secure her husband's estates and the composition of prose and verse. After the Restoration it was her steady habit to dictate metaphysical and philosophical speculations at all hours, and the ladies attending her were compelled (according to Cibber) to sleep near at hand to her Grace in order that at the summons of her bell they might rise instantly during the night to record in writing inspirations which might otherwise have been lost for ever.

The Duchess also produced a Life of her Duke—"no casket is rich enough," says Elia, "no casing sufficiently durable, to honour and keep safe such a jewel"—and some twenty-six plays. Pepys saw one of them, *The Humourous Lovers*, performed in 1667, and thought it the most ridiculous thing that ever was wrote. The handsome Duchess herself aroused no little metaphysical speculation at Court and in the town; she was fantastic in dress as in writing, wore many face-patches, clothed her footmen in velvet, and was virtuous to the point of ill-breeding. She is buried in Westminster Abbey.

Her *Posset for Nature's Breakfast* is remarkable for the romantic comparison of a pair of fair and bashful eyes with a couple of eggs; presumably hard-boiled.

The Body : A Fancy

THE Nerves are France, and Italy, and Spain;
The Liver Britain, the Narrow Sea each Vein;
The Spleen is Aethiopia, wherein
Is bred a people of black and tawny skin;

The Stomach is like Aegypt, and the Chyle,
Which through the body flows, is as the Nile;
The Head and Heart both Indies are; each Ear
Doth like the South and Northern Poles appear;
The Lungs are rocks and caverns, whence rise winds,
Where Life, which passes through, great danger finds.

UPON THE THEME OF LOVE.

No Doubt

ALL that doth flow we cannot liquid name,
Or else would fire and water be the same;
But that is liquid which is moist and wet;
Fire that propriety can never get:
Then 'tis not cold that doth the fire put out,
But 'tis the wet that makes it die, no doubt.

WHAT IS LIQUID.

From "Nature's Dessert"

SWEET marmalade of kisses newly gather'd,
Preserved children, which were newly father'd,
Sugar of Beauty, which away melts soon,
Marchpane of Youth, and childish macaroon:
Sugar-plum words, which fall sweet from the lips,
And water-promises mould'ring like chips;
Biscuits of Love which crumble all away,
Jelly of Fear, which shak'd and quiv'ring lay:
Then was a fresh green-sickness cheese brought in,
And tempting fruit, like that which Eve made sin.

A Posset for Nature's Breakfast

LIFE scums the cream of Beauty with Time's spoon,
And draws the claret-wine of Blushes soon;
Then boils it in a skillet clean of Youth,
And thicks it well with crumbled bread of Truth;

Sets it upon the fire of Life which does
Burn clearer much when Health her bellows blows;
Then takes the eggs of fair and bashful Eyes,
And puts them in a countenance that's wise,
Cuts in a lemon of the sharpest Wit—
Discretion as a knife is used for it—
A handful of chaste Thoughts, double-refined,
Six spoonfuls of a noble and gentle Mind,
A grain of Mirth to give 't a little taste,
Then takes it off for fear the substance waste,
And puts it in a basin of good Health,
And with this meat doth Nature please herself.

E

JOHN DRYDEN (1631–1700)

DRYDEN's reputation is reviving steadily to-day chiefly on account of his prose works, which show him to be one of the foremost modern English critics. Interest in his poetry is more languid, though no highly-quoted modern can display such verse of beaten bronze, such packed wit and sagacity, such vigour, such perpetual epigrammatic splendour as may be found everywhere in his satires. Even his bad or Court verse has a master-ring.

The conceit of Albion's cliffs moving out to sea to meet the King may have been borrowed in essence from a minor French poet, who read it to the great Malherbe and was duly snubbed. That is a quaint fancy, also, of angels drawing back the celestial curtains to peep at the English fleet moving against the Dutch. As for the lines from *Threnodia Augustalis*, they gain a great deal when one remembers how the unfortunate Charles II on his dying-bed was purged, bled, cupped, and blistered by a swarm of doctors for five solid days, according to the precept set forth in that exquisite ballet which ends the *Malade Imaginaire*:

> "*Clysterium donare,*
> *Postea seignare,*
> *Ensuitta purgare,*
> *Reseignare, repurgare, et reclysterisare !*"

The Return of Charles II

THE *Naseby*, now no longer England's shame,
But better to be lost in Charles's name
(Like some unequal bride in nobler sheets),
Receives her lord: the joyful *London* meets

The princely York, himself alone a freight;
The *Swiftsure* groans beneath great Gloster's weight. . . .
The winds that never moderation knew,
Afraid to blow too much, too faintly blew;
Or out of breath with joy could not enlarge
Their straiten'd lungs, or conscious of their charge. . . .

And welcome now, great monarch, to your own;
Behold th' approaching cliffs of Albion!
It is no longer motion cheats your view,
As you meet it, the land approacheth you.
The land returns, and, in the white it wears,
The marks of penitence and sorrow bears.

ASTRÆA REDUX.

The English Fleet Goes Out

IT seems as every ship their sovereign knows,
    His awful summons they so soon obey;
So hear the scaly herd when Proteus blows,
    And so to pasture follow through the sea.

To see this fleet upon the ocean move,
    Angels drew wide the curtains of the skies;
And Heav'n, as if there wanted lights above,
    For tapers made two glaring comets rise.

Whether they unctuous exhalations are,
    Fir'd by the sun, or seeming so alone;
Or each some more remote and slippery star,
    Which loses footing when to mortals shown.

ANNUS MIRABILIS.

The Faculty at Work

THE sons of Art all med'cines tried,
And every noble remedy applied,
With emulation each essay'd
His utmost skill; nay, more, they pray'd:
Never was losing game with better conduct play'd
Death never won a stake with greater toil,
Nor e'er was Fate so near a foil:
But, like a fortress on a rock,
Th' impregnable disease their vain attempts did mock;
They min'd it near, they batter'd from afar
With all the cannon of the med'cinal war;
No gentle means could be essay'd,
'Twas beyond parley when the siege was laid:
Th' extremest ways they first ordain,
Prescribing such intolerable pain
As none but Cæsar could sustain;
Undaunted Cæsar underwent
The malice of their art, nor bent
Beneath whate'er their pious rigour could invent. . . .
Now art was tir'd without success,
No racks could make the stubborn malady confess.
    The vain insurancers of life,
And he who most perform'd and promis'd less,
    Even Short himself, forsook the unequal strife.

THRENODIA AUGUSTALIS.

To Account Rendered

Almeyda. My father's, mother's, brother's deaths I
    pardon:
That's somewhat, sure; a mighty sum of murder,
Of innocent and kindred blood struck off.
My prayers and penance shall discount for these,
And beg of Heaven to charge the bill on me.

DON SEBASTIAN, ACT III.

JOHN BANKS (*fl.* 1677–96)

THE first following extract from the dramatic works of JOHN BANKS, lawyer and unsuccessful Restoration playwright, has been deemed worthy of inclusion if merely for its recording the only blush of Burleigh's known to History.

The lines on Anne Boleyn, also, have (as Henry James said of the musical-comedy star) a certain cadaverous charm.

The Wonder

Cecil. Your Grace is welcome from the Queen of Scotland.
　How fares that sad and most illustrious pattern
　Of all misfortunes?
Norfolk.　　　　　Dost thou pity her?
　Oh, let me fly, and hold thee to my bosom,
　Closer, and far more dear, than ever bride
　Was held by lusty bridegroom in his arms!
Cecil. My lord, you make me blush.

THE ALBION QUEENS, ACT I.

Short Curse

　BE curst the time of Bullen's fatal birth;
　Wrinkles like age anticipate her youth;
　Mildews and blasts devour her wanton beauties;
　Small-pox and leprosy rough-cast her o'er,
　Dig up her charms and features by the roots,
　And bury them in pits as deep as graves.

ANNA BULLEN, ACT I.

33

THOMAS SPRAT (1635–1713)

Dr. Sprat, Bishop of Rochester, man of letters, hedonist, wit, member and historian of the Royal Society, was a charming prelate, a high Tory, and an accomplished host. The charge of pliancy has been brought against him. He certainly preserved urbane relations equally with James II and William III, and he certainly composed with equal literary grace prayers in 1688 for a Prince of Wales and, in the following year, prayers of gratitude for the advent of the Dutchman. His was what is now called a broad, comprehensive standpoint, and he very nearly was appointed Archbishop of York.

Among his works is a biography of his friend Cowley; he also assisted in the revision of Clarendon's monumental history of the Civil Wars. The lament which follows must represent the Absolute Zero of frigidity, and it is difficult to believe that the lover's sighs shook much powder from his great full-bottomed wig.

On His Mistress Drowned

Sweet stream, that dost with equal pace
Both thyself fly, and thyself chase,
　　Forbear awhile to flow,
　　And listen to my woe.
Then go, and tell the sea that all its brine
　　Is fresh, compar'd to mine;
Inform it that the gentle dame,
Who was the life of all my flame,
　　In th' glory of her bud
　　Has pass'd the fatal flood.

34

Death by this only stroke triumphs above
    The greatest power of love:
  Alas, alas! I must give o'er,
  My sighs will let me add no more.

  Go on, sweet stream, and henceforth rest
  No more than does my troubled breast;
And if my sad complaints have made thee stay,
  These tears, these tears shall mend thy way.

JOHN SHEFFIELD, DUKE OF
BUCKINGHAMSHIRE
(1648–1721)

JOHN SHEFFIELD was one of that minority of English peers who behaved as English gentlemen during the Revolution of 1688. While Marlborough, Halifax, Shrewsbury, the bishops, and the rabble of politicians were weeping false tears of joy at the Orangeman's landing, Sheffield remained an active friend to his king, whom they had duped and betrayed. For this Anne made him Lord President of the Council, and George I removed him from office. Sheffield's earlier career was amphibious. In his youth he fought as a volunteer under Rupert, went to sea, and was given command in 1673, after the battle of Southwold Bay, of the *Captain*, the best second-rater in the Fleet which James II founded; in December of the same year he became colonel of the Old Holland Regiment of Foot. He was a friend and patron of Dryden, and himself gave Shakespeare's *Julius Cæsar* a much-needed revision, making it into two separate plays, *Julius Cæsar* and *Marcus Brutus*, and interpolating several interesting love-scenes.

His verse is good stout colonel's work, and he rides Pegasus on the snaffle. His picture of King David kindly looking over and correcting Purcell's consecutive fifths in Paradise is not unattractive.

Heavy Going

FROM mighty Cæsar, and his boundless grace,
Tho' Brutus once, at least, his life receiv'd,
Such obligations, tho' so high believ'd,
    Are yet but slight in such a case.
Where friendship so possesses all the place,
There is no room for gratitude, since he,

Who so obliges, is more pleas'd than his sav'd friend
    can be. . . .
From such a friendship unprovok'd to fall
Is horrid, yet I wish the fact were all,
Which does with too much cause ungrateful Brutus
    call. . . .

    He whom thus Brutus doom'd to bleed,
      Did, setting his own race aside,
        Nothing less for him provide,
    Than in the world's great empire to succeed;
    Which we are bound in justice to allow
      Is all-sufficient proof to show
That Brutus did not strike for his own sake:
And if, alas, he fail'd, 'twas only by mistake.

                  On Brutus, an Ode.

The Blue Pencil

Good angels snatch'd him eagerly on high;
Joyful they flew, and soaring through the sky,
    Teaching his new-fledg'd soul to fly;
    While we, alas! lamenting lie.
    He went musing all along,
      Composing new their heavenly song:
Awhile his skilful notes loud hallelujahs drown'd;
But soon they ceas'd their own, to catch his pleasing
    sound.
David himself improv'd the harmony,
David, in sacred story so renown'd
No less for music, than for poetry! . . .
If human cares are lawful to the blest,
Already settled in eternal rest,
Needs must he wish, that Purcell only might
Have liv'd to set what he vouchsaf'd to write.

     Ode on the Death of Mr. Henry Purcell.

NAHUM TATE (1652–1715)

NAHUM TATE, son of Mr. Faithful Teate, a worthy vessel, graduated at Trinity College, Dublin (in whose rolls he appears as "Teate"), and came to London, publishing a volume of poetry in 1677. His version of *King Lear*, by Shakespeare, invites comparison with a recent interesting Hollywood revision of *The Taming of the Shrew*, for Mr. Tate cut the Fool out altogether and allowed Cordelia to marry Edgar. He became Poet Laureate in 1692, and in 1696 produced, with Brady, the well-known doggerel version of the Psalms of David. His verse is for the most part adulatory and elegiac. He was an honest dull man, downcast in expression and given, says his biographer, to fuddling. His creditors pursued the honest man in 1715, and he died in hiding from them.

Pope was severe:

> "And he who now to Sense, and now to Nonsense leaning,
> Means not, but blunders round about a Meaning,
> And he whose Fustian's so sublimely bad,
> It is not Poetry, but Prose run mad:
> All these my modest Satire bade translate,
> And own'd that nine such Poets made a TATE."

Ode upon the New Year

(1693)

THE happy, happy year is born,
    That wonders shall disclose;
That conquest with fix'd laurels shall adorn,
And give our lab'ring Hercules repose.
    Ye Graces that resort
To Virtue's temple, blest Maria's court,
    With incense and with songs as sweet
    The long-expected season meet,
    The long-expected season gently greet.

Maria (thus devoutly say)—
Maria—oh, appear, appear!
Thy softest charms display.
Smile and bless the infant year;
Smile on its birth in kindness to our isle.
For if this genial day
You cheerfully survey,
Succeeding years in just return on you and us shall smile.

Thus let departing Winter sing:
Approach, advance, thou promis'd Spring,
And if for action not design'd,
Together, soon, together bring
Confederate troops in Europe's cause combin'd.
A busier prospect Summer yields,
Floating navies, harass'd fields,
From far the Gallic genius spying
(Of unjust war the just disgrace),
Their broken squadrons flying,
And Britain's Cæsar light'ning in the chase.

SIR RICHARD BLACKMORE (*d.* 1729)

WHAT hours RICHARD BLACKMORE, M.D., snatched from professional duties he devoted to prose and poetry alike—for he was indifferent. His first work, *Prince Arthur, an Heroick Poem in Ten Books*, was composed, he says, "for the greater Part in Coffee-Houses, or in passing up and down the Streets." In 1697 he was knighted by William III and appointed Royal Physician, though his personal charm seems to have been negligible. A *Short History of the Last Parliament* followed in 1699; and from now till his death Sir Richard wrote freely. He wrote octavos on Wit, on the Nature of Man (a Poem, in Three Books), on Eliza (an Epic Poem, in Ten Books), on the Creation, on the Arian Hypothesis, on the Plague, on Alfred (an Epic Poem, in Twelve Books), on the Dropsy, on the Psalms, on the Conspiracy against the Person and Government of King William III, on the Redemption (a Divine Poem, in Six Books), on the Gout, and on Natural Theology, or Moral Duties considered apart from Positive. He wrote Essays on Several Subjects, and Poems on the Same. He wrote Paraphrases of the Book of Job and the Psalms of David, and a Critical Dissertation on the Spleen. He left for posthumous publication *The Accomplish'd Preacher, or, an Essay on Divine Eloquence*. He was a writer whom nothing could daunt, and is justly encrusted in *The Dunciad*:

> "All hail him Victor in both Gifts of Song,
> Who sings so loudly, and who sings so long."

Of the extracts which follow some were singled out by Martinus Scriblerus for comment in his *Art of Sinking*. The paraphrase of Psalm CIV, in which Almighty God is shown unrolling a pile of ether ("*Now this,*" *said Mr. Trabb, taking down a roll of cloth and tiding it out in a flowing manner over the counter,* "*is a very sweet article*"), is commendable: also the picture of the illuminations in heaven, in which the celestial citizens celebrate the Creator (says Scriblerus) "by huzzaing, making illuminations, and flinging squibs, crackers, and sky-rockets," as on Lord Mayor's Day.

The Chase of the Metaphor

THE stones and all the elements with thee
Shall ratify a strict confederacy;
Wild beasts their savage temper shall forget,
And for a firm alliance with thee treat;
The finny tyrant of the spacious seas
Shall send a scaly embassy for peace;
His plighted faith the crocodile shall keep,
And seeing thee, for joy sincerely weep.

JOB.

From the Psalms

I

HE measures all the drops with wondrous skill,
Which the black clouds, His floating bottles, fill.

PSALM CIV.

II

Didst Thou one end of air's wide curtain hold,
And help the bales of ether to unfold?
Say, which cærulean pile was by Thy hand unroll'd?

IBID.

From the Book of Job

I

I CANNOT stifle this gigantick woe,
Nor on my raging grief a muzzle throw.

II

All Nature felt a reverential shock,
The sea stood still to see the mountains rock.

III

With teats distended with their milky store,
Such num'rous lowing herds, before my door,
Their painful burden to unload did meet,
That we with butter might have wash'd our feet.

The Crystal Palaces

GLORIOUS illuminations, made on high
By all the stars and planets of the sky,
In just degrees and shining order plac'd,
Spectators charm'd, and the blest dwelling grac'd.
Through all th' enlighten'd air swift fireworks flew,
Which with repeated shouts glad cherubs threw.
Comets ascended with their sweeping train,
Then fell in starry show'rs and glitt'ring rain.
In air ten thousand meteors blazing hung,
Which from th' eternal battlements were flung.

PRINCE ARTHUR.

Possibilities

I

IF casual concourse did the world compose,
And things from hits fortuitous arose,
Then anything might come from anything;
For how from chance can constant order spring?
The forest oak might bear the blushing rose,
And fragrant myrtles thrive in Russian snows;
The fair pomegranate might adorn the pine,
The grape the bramble, and the sloe the vine;
Fish from the plains, birds from the floods, might rise,
And lowing herds break from the starry skies.

THE CREATION, BK. III.

Omar Khayyam

II

In the wide womb of possibility
Lie many things, which ne'er may actual be;
And more productions, of a various kind,
Will cause no contradictions in the mind.
'Tis possible the things in Nature found,
Might different forms and different parts have own'd:
The bear might wear a trunk, the wolf a horn,
The peacock's train the bittern might adorn;
Strong tusks might in the horse's mouth have grown,
And lions might have spots, and leopards none.

Ibid., Bk. V.

JOSEPH ADDISON (1672–1719)

OF ADDISON it may be perpetually said, echoing Thackeray, that "it is as a Tatler of small-talk and a Spectator of mankind that we cherish and love him, and owe as much pleasure to him as to any human being that ever wrote." It was as a poet that he burst into public fame, quite suddenly, when the Earl of Godolphin, an excellent judge of race-horses, highly approved an ode on Marlborough's victory at Blenheim which the Ministry wanted written—for in that Arcadian age poetry was so ordered—and which Mr. Addison had been commissioned to supply. The ode was left unfinished at a striking passage comparing John Churchill with an Angel of God, and Mr. Addison immediately appointed Commissioner of Appeals, and later, in succession, Under-Secretary of State, Secretary to the Lord-Lieutenant of Ireland, and one of the Principal Secretaries of State.

He had his minor blemishes: he was a prig; he was excessively insular; he was fat; he was king of a London literary clique; he behaved badly to Steele; his blood was chilly. He called young Lord Warwick to his bedside to "see how a Christian could die"; unluckily, adds Horace Walpole, he died of brandy. And if his prose is exquisite his verse (which he ranked far above his essays) is almost uniformly mediocre or bad. He is said to have been annoyed when his colleague in opera, Clayton, the composer, expanded the last line of King Henry's song to "Oh, the pleasing, pleasing, pleasing, pleasing anguish" —thus doubling the pleasure without authority. Nevertheless Addison could laugh mildly at himself in a *Guardian* paper, parodying contemporary operatic librettists in a lyric beginning:

> "Oh, the charming month of May,
> Oh, the charming month of May,
> When the breezes fan the treeses,
> Full of blossoms fresh and gay!"

Rosamond's Song

From walk to walk, from shade to shade,
From stream to purling stream convey'd,
Through all the mazes of the grove,
Through all the mingling tracts I rove,
      Turning,
      Burning,
      Changing,
      Ranging,
Full of grief and full of love,
Impatient for my lord's return
I sigh, I pine, I rave, I mourn.
Was ever passion cross'd like mine?
      To rend my breast,
      And break my rest,
A thousand ills combine.
      Absence wounds me,
      Fear surrounds me,
      Guilt confounds me,
Was ever passion cross'd like mine?

How does my constant grief deface
The pleasures of this happy place!
In vain the spring my senses greets,
In all her colours, all her sweets;
      To me the rose
      No longer glows,
      Every plant
      Has lost his scent;
The vernal blooms of various hue,
The blossoms fresh with morning dew,
The breeze, that sweeps these fragrant bowers,
Fill'd with the breath of op'ning flowers,
      Purple scenes,
      Winding greens,
      Glooms inviting,
      Birds delighting

F

(Nature's softest, sweetest store),
Charm my tortur'd soul no more.
Ye powers, I rave, I faint, I die:
Why so slow, great Henry, why?
    From death and alarms
    Fly, fly to my arms,
Fly to my arms, my monarch, fly!

                     ROSAMOND, ACT I, Sc. IV.

King Henry's Song

OH, the pleasing, pleasing anguish,
When we love, and when we languish!
    Wishes rising!
    Thoughts surprising!
    Pleasure courting!
    Charms transporting!
    Fancy viewing
    Joys ensuing!
Oh, the pleasing, pleasing anguish!

                     IBID., Sc. VI.

ISAAC WATTS (1674–1748)

DR. WATTS, the celebrated hymnodist, was for a great part of his life minister to the wealthy dissenting congregation of Mark Lane Chapel, in the City. The luxurious comfort and quiet of Theobalds, where he lived some thirty-five years as the guest of Sir Thomas and Lady Abney, did much to preserve his health, which was not good. Watts's writings exhale for the most part a mild and sentimental adaptation of Calvinism; for he was a good man, and shrank from the terrible conclusions of Calvin's French logic. His free adaptation of the Psalms (1719) is remarkable chiefly for the substitution of "Britain" for "Israel," which links the poet with those retired Anglo-Indian colonels in Cheltenham of our own day who prove conclusively that we are the Lost Tribes.

A brief note on the subjects of the lines following may increase the reader's pleasure. Thomas Gunston, Esq., Lady Abney's brother, died in 1700, "when he had just finished his Seat at *Newington*"; hence his especial interest in the architecture of Heaven. The second visitor to Paradise is Dr. Watts's grandfather, one of Blake's commanders, who was blown up in an explosion aboard his ship; he was a capable linguist, as the verse records, and also found much to interest him above. Mr. Matthew Mead, Mr. William Bates, and Mr. Thomas Gouge were dissenting ministers of whom the anger of Heaven deprived England, for her sins, in 1699–1700. Mrs. Anne Warner, whose search for a suitable heavenly mansion to let enhances her housewifely reputation, was a friend of the poet's. The detachment of angels on night-duty during her ascension, as Dr. Watts elsewhere records:

> "The midnight watch of angels, that patrol
> The British sky, have noticed her ascent
> Near the meridian star,"

was no doubt furnished by the brigade of angels paraded to welcome William of Orange—not to speak of the rouged and dainty young Dutchmen his loves—on his landing on these shores. It seems likely that this angelic brigade, obeying Dr. Watts's command, took up permanent quarters at White-hall with William, and—such is British conservatism and such is red tape—is possibly still "on the strength."

Mr. Gunston is Shown round Heaven

GENTLE Ithuriel led him round the skies,
The buildings struck him with immense surprise;
The spires all radiant and the mansions bright,
The roof high-vaulted with ethereal light. . . .
Millions of glories reign through every part;
Infinite power, and uncreated art,
Stand here display'd, and to the stranger show
How it outshines the noblest seats below.
The stranger fed his gazing powers awhile
Transported: then, with a regardless smile,
Glanc'd his eye downward through the crystal floor,
And took eternal leave of what he built before.

TO THE DEAR MEMORY OF
THOMAS GUNSTON, ESQ.

A Polyglot in Paradise

RECOUNT the years, my song (a mournful round!),
    Since he was seen on earth no more;
    He fought in lower seas and drown'd;
    But victory and peace are found
        On the superior shore.
There now his tuneful breath in sacred songs
Employs the European and the Eastern tongues.

ON THE DEATH OF AN
AGED AND HONOURED RELATIVE

Mr. Mead, Mr. Bates, and Mr. Gouge

HEAVEN was impatient of our crimes,
    And sent his minister of death
To scourge the bold rebellion of the times,
    And to demand our prophet's breath;
He came commission'd for the fates
Of awful Mead and charming Bates;
There he essayed the vengeance first,
Then took a dismal aim, and brought great Gouge to dust.

AN ELEGY ON MR. THOMAS GOUGE.

Mrs. Warner Arrives Above

BEHOLD her ancestors (a pious race),
Rang'd in fair order, at her sight rejoice,
And sing her welcome.   She along their seats
Gliding salutes them all with honours due,
Such as are paid in Heaven: and last she finds
A mansion fashion'd of distinguish'd light,
But vacant; "This," with sure presage she cries,
"Awaits my father; when will he arrive?
How long, alas, how long!"   Then calls her mate:
"Die, thou dear partner of my mortal cares,
Die, and partake my bliss; we are for ever one."

AN ELEGIAC THOUGHT ON
MRS. ANNE WARNER.

On the Landing of William III

BUT lo! the great Deliverer sails,
Commission'd from Jehovah's hand,
And smiling seas, and wishing gales,
Convey him to the longing land.

Brigades of angels lin'd the way,
And guarded William to his throne;
There, ye celestial warriors, stay,
And make his palace like your own.

Then, mighty God! the earth shall know
And learn the worship of the sky;
Angels and Britons join below,
To raise their hallelujahs high.

A HYMN OF PRAISE FOR
THREE GREAT SALVATIONS.

COLLEY CIBBER (1671–1757)

Mr. Cibber, comedian, dramatist, poet, Mr. Cibber of the Theatre Royal, Haymarket, and Drury Lane, Mr. Cibber, panegyrist of the House of Hanover, took his fair share in the brawling and scuffling of the sons of the Muses. Pope, Gay, and Fielding attacked him, Steele and Lord Chesterfield were his friends, and his inordinate vanity armed him with triple brass. "No creature smarts so little as a Fool," observes the redoubtable Mr. Pope:

> "Whom have I hurt? Has Poet yet, or Peer,
> Lost the arch'd Eye-brow, or Parnassian Sneer?
> And has not Colley still his Lord, and Whore?"

Johnson, however, in his pontifical way, acquits Cibber of being a blockhead. He was undoubtedly a great comedy actor, his *Apology* is the most entertaining of autobiographies, and one or two of his plays are not without merit—for example *Love's Last Shift*, which according to the ripe old story was once rendered into the French as *La Dernière Chemise de l'Amour*. Cibber's strong attachment to Hanover (his father was a native of Flensborg) produced the odes which follow. In one of them Almighty God and George II are seen amicably sharing the empire of Britain, in the other George is perceived to be the crowning glory and sole *raison d'être* of the Creation; and one must needs admire the poet's tough struggle to get Seligenstadt, Klein-Ostein, Aschaffenburg, and Dettingen into an "Air." As Swift said:

> "In vain are all attempts from Germany
> To find out proper words for harmony."

From the New Year's Ode, 1731

Air

Ye grateful Britons, bless the year
   That kindly yields increase,
While plenty that might feed a war
   Enjoys the guard of Peace.
Your plenty to the Skies you owe,
   Peace is your Monarch's care,
Thus bounteous Jove and George below
   Divided empire share.

Recitative

Britannia, pleas'd, looks round her realms to see
Your various causes of felicity!
(To glorious War, a glorious Peace succeeds:
For most we triumph when the farmer feeds.)
Then truly are we great when truth supplies
Our blood, our treasures drain'd by victories.
Turn, happy Britons, to the throne your eyes,
   And in the royal offspring see
How amply bounteous Providence supplies
   The source of your felicity.

Air

Behold in ev'ry face imperial graces shine!
All native to the race of George and Caroline.
   In each young hero we admire
   The blooming virtues of his sire;
   In each maturing fair we find
   Maternal charms of softer kind.

Recitative

In vain thro' ages past has Phœbus roll'd
Ere such a sight blest Albion could behold.
Thrice happy mortals, if your state you knew,

Where can the globe so blest a nation shew?
All that of you indulgent Heav'n requires,
Is loyal hearts, to reach your own desires.
Let Faction then her self-born views lay down,
And hearts united thus address the throne:

Air

Hail! Royal Cæsar, hail!
Like this may ev'ry annual sun
Add brighter glories to thy crown,
  Till suns themselves shall fail.

From the Birthday Ode, 1732

LET there be light!
Such was at once the word and work of Heav'n,
  When from the void of universal night
  Free nature sprung to the Creator's sight,
And day to glad the new-born world was giv'n.

Succeeding days to ages roll'd,
And ev'ry age some wonder told:
At length arose this glorious morn!
  When, to extend his bounteous pow'r,
  High Heav'n announc'd this instant hour
The best of monarchs shall be born! . . .

The word that form'd the world
  In vain did make mankind;
Unless, his passions to restrain,
  Almighty wisdom had design'd
Sometimes a WILLIAM, or a GEORGE should reign
Yet farther, *Britons*, cast your eyes,
  Behold a long succession rise
  Of future fair felicities.

Around the royal table spread,
See how the beauteous branches shine!
   Sprung from the fertile genial bed
Of glorious GEORGE and CAROLINE.
   While Heav'n with bounteous hand
Has so enrich'd her store;
   When shall this promis'd land
In royal heirs be poor?
   All we can further ask, or Heav'n bestow,
Is, that we long this happiness may know.

From Another, 1743

OF fields, of forts, and floods, unknown to fame,
That now demand of Cæsar's arms a name,
   Sing, Britons, tho' uncouth the sound.

Air

   Tho' rough Seligenstadt
   The harmony defeat,
Tho' Klein-Ostein the verse confound;
   Yet, in the joyful strain,
   Aschaffenburgh or Dettingen
Shall charm the ear they seem to wound.

AMBROSE PHILIPS (1675–1749)

Ambrose Philips ("Namby Pamby"), a friend of Swift and Addison and an enemy of Pope, has suffered for his lines to little Margaret Pulteney and other well-born infants which Henry Carey parodied:

> "Let the verse the subject fit,
> Little subject, little wit,
> Namby Pamby is your guide,
> Albion's joy, Hibernia's pride" (*etc.*).

Actually he was a minor poet of some sensibility, and, his red stockings and dandified air apart, no coxcomb, though Swift once described him to Stella as "more a puppy than ever," and Johnson said that his works were "not loaded with thought." A performance of his tragedy, *The Distrest Mother* —a barbarous handling of *Andromaque*—at which Sir Roger de Coverley was present, provided Mr. Spectator with a choice paper. Like other happy sons of Apollo in his time Philips held lucrative public office, being secretary to the Lord Chancellor and a judge of the Prerogative Court.

His very sensible tribute to Property, goddess of English birth, was written in 1714, when the financial situation appeared to be relieved by the ousting of the heirs to the English throne in favour of the German succession. It would be substantially approved by Tennyson's farmer:

> "Wot's a beauty?—the flower as blaws.
> But proputty, proputty sticks, an' proputty, proputty graws."

Compare in this matter the sentiments of Mr. Thomas Warton, *post*.

Salute to Property

But who advances next, with cheerful grace,
Joy in her eye, and plenty in her face?
A wheaten garland does her head adorn:
O Property! O goddess, English-born!

Where hast thou been? How did the wealthy mourn!
The bankrupt nation sighed for thy return,
Doubtful for whom her spreading funds were fill'd,
Her fleets were freighted, and her fields were till'd.

To THE RIGHT HON.
CHARLES LORD HALIFAX.

Ode

*To Miss Margaret Pulteney, Daughter of Daniel
Pulteney, Esq., in the Nursery*

DIMPLY damsel, sweetly smiling,
All caressing, none beguiling,
Bud of beauty, fairly blowing,
Every charm to nature owing,
This and that new thing admiring,
Much of this and that inquiring,
Knowledge by degrees attaining,
Day by day some virtue gaining,
Ten years hence, when I leave chiming,
Beardless poets, fondly rhyming
(Fescu'd now, perhaps, in spelling),
On thy riper beauties dwelling,
Shall accuse each killing feature
Of the cruel, charming creature,
Whom I know complying, willing,
Tender, and averse to killing

To the Right Hon. Robert Walpole, Esq.

15 *June*, 1724

VOTARY to public zeal,
Minister of England's weal,
Have you leisure for a song,
Tripping lightly o'er the tongue,
Swift and sweet in every measure,

Tell me, Walpole, have you leisure?
Nothing lofty will I sing,
Nothing of the favourite king,
Something, rather, sung with ease,
Simply elegant to please.
    Fairy virgin, British Muse,
Some unheard-of story choose:
Choose the glory of the swain,
Gifted with a magic strain,
Swaging grief of every kind,
Healing, with a verse, the mind:
To him came a man of power,
To him, in a cheerless hour;
When the swain, by Druids taught,
Soon divin'd his irksome thought,
Soon the maple harp he strung,
Soon with silver-accent, sung.

JOHN, LORD HERVEY (1696–1743)

Of Lord Hervey of Ickworth, Hervey of the painted cheeks, the *mœurs spéciales*, and the coffin-face, Pope's "Lord Fanny" and "Sporus," it may be justly said that he was a type of politician worthy of rubbing shoulders with his predecessors the Cecils and Russells and others who sprang into power from the plunder of the English Monasteries, and like them entirely free from scruple, faith, or morals. He ratted in the ordinary manner from the Opposition for a pension of a thousand a year, deserting Pulteney for Walpole, whom George II had taken for Prime Minister. Pulteney nearly ran him through in a duel in the Green Park in 1731, but Hervey lived to be Lord Privy Seal and to cling to office through thick and thin, diseased as he was: "as full," said Horace Walpole in 1742, a year before Hervey's death, "of his dirty little politics as ever." Thackeray's amiable horror at the perusal of Hervey's Memoirs, published at his express order a hundred years after his death, provides a characteristic passage in *The Four Georges*.

Of the effusions of Hervey's Muse which follow, the first is even more engaging than Canning's well-known parody:

> "The feathered tribes on pinions swim the air;
> Not so the Mackerel:—and still less the Bear."

The second is as reasoned a plea for farmyard morals as any advanced thinker of to-day could desire.

Nature Queries

I

Will the wise Elephant desert the wood,
To imitate the whale and range the flood?
Or will the Mole her native earth forsake,
In wanton madness to explore the lake?

II

Would any feather'd maiden of the wood,
Or scaly female of the peopled flood,
When lust and hunger call'd, its force resist?
In abstinence or chastity persist?
And cry, "If Heaven's intent were understood,
These tastes were only given to be withstood"?
Or would they wisely both these gifts improve,
And eat when hungry, and when am'rous love?

EPISTLE TO MR. FOX, FROM HAMPTON COURT.

JOHN ARMSTRONG (1709–79)

JOHN ARMSTRONG, M.D., a Scottish physician, added (like Blackmore) fresh uneasiness to his patients' normal misgivings by indulging himself in poetry. His was not in any case a character exuding the vague optimism which the English love. He had, as Beattie wrote to Forbes, "a rooted aversion against the whole human Race, except a few Friends, which it seems are dead"; and to this splenetic Swift-like temper he added an habitual inertness. His first poetical work, *The Œconomy of Love* (1736), was anonymous, and curtly dismissed by Dr. Johnson. It was followed, cynically enough to delight a Voltaire, by a prose *Synopsis of the History and Cure of Venereal Diseases*. The publication of *Benevolence : an Epistle* added little to his literary reputation, which was not high; it was followed by *Taste : an Epistle to Young Critics*. He became in 1760 a physician to the British Army in Germany, and later retired. To the surprise of his friends he left on his death the sum of three thousand pounds.

Armstrong's *Art of Preserving Health*, from which the following extracts are taken, enriched our heritage of English Poetry with a relentless analysis of the workings of the human stomach. The description of a rustic interior (*O dura messorum ilia !*) is peculiarly vivid, and the poet's advice to those of "jovial make" is perceptibly tinged with gloomy pleasure at their sufferings. He advises washing, in moderation. The Age of Reason, indeed, had no passion for the bath. As to feather-beds, he permits them chiefly—if one may translate correctly from the text—to company-promoters and drunkards. But one may forgive him anything, even:

> "For from the colliquation of soft joys
>   How changed you rise! the ghost of what you was!"

for the sake of:

> "that divinest gift,
>   The gay, serene, good-natured Burgundy."

60

Rustic Interior

NOTHING so foreign but th' athletic hind
Can labour into blood.   The hungry meal
Alone he fears, or aliments too thin;
By violent powers too easily subdued,
Too soon expelled.   His daily labour thaws,
To friendly chyle, the most rebellious mass
That salt can harden, or the smoke of years;
Nor does his gorge the luscious bacon rue,
Nor that which Cestria sends, tenacious paste
Of solid milk.[1]   But ye of softer clay,
Infirm and delicate! and ye who waste
With pale and bloated sloth the tedious day!
Avoid the stubborn aliment, avoid
The full repast; and let sagacious age
Grow wiser, lesson'd by the dropping teeth.

ART OF PRESERVING HEALTH, BK. II.

Advice to the Stout

THE languid stomach curses even the pure
Delicious fat, and all the race of oil:
For more the oily aliments relax
Its feeble tone; and with the eager lymph
(Fond to incorporate with all it meets)
Coyly they mix, and shun with slippery wiles
The woo'd embrace.   The irresoluble oil,
So gentle late and blandishing, in floods
Of rancid bile o'erflows: what tumults hence,
What horrors rise, were nauseous to relate.
Choose leaner viands, ye whose jovial make
Too fast the gummy nutriment imbibes.

IBID.

[1] i.e. Cheshire cheese.

G

The Gastric Muse

THERE are, whose blood
Impetuous rages through the turgid veins,
Who better bear the fiery fruits of Ind
Than the moist melon, or pale cucumber.
Of chilly nature others fly the board
Supplied with slaughter, and the vernal powers
For cooler, kinder, sustenance implore.
Some even the generous nutriment detest
Which, in the shell, the sleeping embryo rears.
Some, more unhappy still, repent the gifts
Of Pales; soft, delicious and benign: . . .
The fostering dew of tender sprouting life;
The best refection of declining age. . . .

The stomach, urged beyond its active tone,
Hardly to nutrimental chyle subdues
The softest food: unfinished and depraved,
The chyle, in all its future wand'rings, owns
Its turbid fountain; not by purer streams
So to be cleared, but foulness will remain.

IBID.

On Washing

AGAINST the rigours of a damp cold heaven
To fortify their bodies, some frequent
The gelid cistern; and, where naught forbids,
I praise their dauntless heart. . . .
Let those who from the frozen Arctos reach
Parched Mauritania, or the sultry West,
Or the wide flood that laves rich Indostan,
Plunge thrice a day, and in the tepid wave
Untwist their stubborn pores: that full and free
Th' evaporation through the softened skin
May bear proportion to the swelling blood.

So may they 'scape the fever's rapid flames;
So feel untainted the hot breath of hell.
With us, the man of no complaint demands
The warm ablution just enough to keep
The body sacred from indecent soil.
Still to be pure, even did it not conduce
(As much it does) to health, were greatly worth
Your daily pains.   'Tis this adorns the rich;
The want of this is poverty's worst woe;
With this external virtue age maintains
A decent grace; without it, youth and charms
Are loathsome.   This the venal Graces know;
So doubtless do your wives: for married sires,
As well as lovers, still pretend to taste;
Nor is it less (all prudent wives can tell)
To lose a husband's than a lover's heart.

Ibid., Bk. III.

On Feather Beds

Ye prone to sleep (whom sleeping most annoys),
On the hard mattress or elastic couch
Extend your limbs, and wean yourselves from sloth;
Nor grudge the lean projector, of dry brain
And springy nerves, the blandishments of down:
Nor envy while the buried bacchanal
Exhales his surfeit in prolixer dreams.

Ibid.

EDWARD YOUNG (1683–1765)

"HARK to the d—d sycophantic son of a —— of a parson,"
observed Fielding of Warburton at Ralph Allen's table. This
considered judgment may also serve to sum up the major
tendencies and preoccupations of the Rev. Dr. EDWARD YOUNG,
a man admittedly of considerable parts as epigrammatist, critic,
and satirist, whose *Night Thoughts* enjoyed European celebrity
(it was Robespierre's bed-book), who made three thousand
pounds by a collection of satires, and whose long life was spent
in congees and salamalecs before the Whigs, the Tories, and the
Court alike, and in hunting preferment as a pig hunts truffles.
Dr. Young made his début as a member of Addison's literary
court. In 1726, having been assiduous in the company of
such politicians as Bubb Dodington, Lord Melbourne, and
Walpole, he was awarded a pension of two hundred pounds
from the Ministry; in 1728 he became a chaplain to the King;
from 1730 onwards he began complaining about the meagre
results of his sycophancy. In 1730 he received the good living
of Welwyn, Hertfordshire, and married a daughter of the
Earl of Lichfield; in 1742 he published *Night Thoughts* and
was hailed an ornament to Religion and Letters. In 1746,
and at intervals till 1758, although very rich, he was still
complaining to the Duke of Newcastle and other influential
persons; but the rainbow's end eluded him to the last, and
the Prince of Wales steadily ignored his claims. In 1761 he
was appointed Clerk of the Closet to the Princess Dowager,
which was gratifying, but hollow. He died in April 1765.

Young's lyric verse for the most part mingles bombast, adula-
tion, bathos, and platitude in equal measure. His ode prefacing
Ocean and addressed to George II, and *Ocean* itself, show what
he can do in the way of shoe-buckle kissing. To a modern
taste there is a deal of unconscious gaiety in the Ode on
the Assembly of Parliament calling on the nations to tremble
at the meeting of Britain's awful Senate. Young is the
Kipling of his time, trumpeting in addition the glories of Big

Business like a poetic Callisthenes. Observe the note in such lines as:

> "By Jove, by Fame,
>   By GEORGE's name,
> Awake! awake! awake! awake!"

and:

> "Wake, sting her up!—Trade! lean no more
>   On thy fix'd anchor; push from shore";

and observe with what justice and propriety the lines on Parliament:

> "The walls, the very walls advise,
>   Each mean, degenerate thought chastise,
> And rouse the sons with all their fathers' fires,"

may be still recited wherever there are rude echoes of Marconi share scandals. And finally, let the attractive vignette of Britannia shocking the Continent ("*schoking !*" as the French are wont to say, with their sardonic glance across the Channel) be duly noted for its unexpectedness.

A Submarine Jaunt

As yawns an earthquake, when imprison'd air
Struggles for vent, and lays the centre bare,
The whale extends his jaws' enormous size;
The Prophet views the cavern with surprise;
Measures his monstrous teeth, afar descried,
And rolls his wond'ring eyes from side to side:
Then takes possession of the spacious seat,
And sails secure within the dark retreat.

THE LAST DAY.

Seascape

BUT though full noble is my theme,
  Full urgent is my call
To soften sorrow, and forbid
  The bursting tear to fall:

The task I dread; dare I to leave
    Of humble prose the shore,
And put to sea? a dangerous sea?
    What throngs have sunk before!

How proud the poet's billow swells!
    The God! the God! his boast:
A boast how vain!   What wrecks abound!
    Dead bards stench every coast.

RESIGNATION, PART I.

A Runcible Thought [1]

O! HOW disorder'd our machine,
    When contradictions mix!
When Nature strikes no less than twelve,
    And Folly points at six!

To mend the movements of your heart,
    How great is my delight!
Gently to wind your morals up
    And set your hand aright!

IBID., PART II.

"Sting Her Up!"

WHERE, Industry, thy daughter fair?
    Recall her to her native air:
Here was Trade born, here bred, here flourish'd long;
    And ever shall she flourish here.
    What, though she languish'd? 'twas but fear:
She's sound of heart, her constitution strong.

[1] Addressed to the poet's "dear friend, Voltaire," then in
his sixty-eighth year and quite incorrigible.

Wake, sting her up!—Trade! lean no more
On thy fix'd anchor; push from shore:
Earth lies before thee; every climate court.
And see, she's rous'd, absolv'd from fears,
Her brow in cloudless azure rears,
Spreads all her sail, and opens every port.

See, cherish'd by her sister, Peace,
She levies gain on every place,
Religion, habit, custom, tongue, and name.
Again she travels with the sun,
Again she draws a golden zone
Round earth and main,—bright zone of wealth and fame!

IMPERIUM PELAGI, OR, THE MERCHANT.

From the "Ode to the King"

[*Prefixed to "Ocean"*]

OLD Ocean's praise
Demands my lays;
A truly British theme I sing;
A theme so great,
I dare compete,
And join with Ocean, Ocean's King. . . .

The naval crown
Is all his own!
Our fleet, if war, or commerce, call,
His will performs
Through waves and storms
And rides in triumph round the ball.

No former race,
With strong embrace,
This theme to ravish durst aspire;
With virgin charms
My soul it warms,
And melts melodious on my lyre. . . .

On yonder height
What golden light
Triumphant shines? and shines alone?
Unrivall'd blaze!
The nations gaze!
'Tis not the sun; 'tis Britain's throne.

Our monarch, there,
Rear'd high in air,
Should tempests rise, disdains to bend,
Like British oak,
Derides the stroke;
His blooming honours far extend!

Beneath them lies,
With lifted eyes,
Fair Albion, like an amorous maid;
While interest wings
Bold foreign kings
To fly, like eagles, to his shade.

At his proud foot
The sea, pour'd out,
Immortal nourishment supplies;
Thence wealth and state,
And power and fate,
Which Europe reads in GEORGE's eyes.

From what we view,
We take the clue,
Which leads from great to greater things:
Men doubt no more,
But gods adore,
When such resemblance shines in kings!

From "Ocean, an Ode"

WHO sings the source
   Of wealth and force?
Vast fields of commerce, and big war,
   Where wonders dwell!
   Where terrors swell!
And Neptune thunders from his car?

   Where? where are they,
   Whom Pæan's ray
Has touch'd, and bid divinely rave?—
   What! none aspire?
   I snatch the lyre,
And plunge into the foaming wave.

   The wave resounds!
   The rock rebounds!
The Nereids to my song reply!
   I lead the choir,
   And they conspire,
With voice and shell, to lift it high. . . .

   The main! the main!
   Is Britain's reign;
Her strength, her glory, is her fleet:
   The main! the main!
   Be Britain's strain;
As Triton's strong, as Siren's sweet.

   Thro' nature wide
   Is nought descried
So rich in pleasure or surprise;
   When all-serene,
   How sweet the scene!
How dreadful, when the billows rise;

And storms deface
The fluid glass
In which erewhile Britannia fair
Look'd down with pride,
Like Ocean's bride,
Adjusting her majestic air! . . .

The northern blast,
The shatter'd mast,
The syrt, the whirlpool, and the rock,
The breaking spout,
The stars gone out,
The boiling strait, the monster's shock,

Let others fear;
To Britain dear
Whate'er promotes her daring claim;
Those terrors charm,
Which keep her warm
In chase of honest gain, or fame. . . .

From Indian mines,
With proud designs,
The merchant, swoln, digs golden ore;
The tempests rise,
And seize the prize,
And toss him breathless on the shore.

His son complains
In pious strains,
"Ah, cruel thirst of gold!" he cries;
Then ploughs the main
In zeal for gain,
The tears yet swelling in his eyes.

Thou wat'ry vast!
What mounds are cast
To bar thy dreadful flowings o'er!
Thy proudest foam
Must know its home;
But rage of gold disdains a shore. . . .

Ye warlike slain!
Beneath the main,
Wrapt in a wat'ry winding-sheet;
Who bought with blood
Your country's good,
Your country's full-blown glory meet.

What pow'rful charm
Can death disarm?
Your long, your iron slumbers break?
By Jove, by Fame,
By GEORGE's name,
Awake! awake! awake! awake!

With spiral shell,
Full blasted, tell,
That all your wat'ry realms should ring;
Your pearl alcoves,
Your coral groves,
Should echo theirs, and Britain's King.

As long as stars
Guide mariners,
As Carolina's virtues please,
Or suns invite
The ravish'd sight,
The British flag shall sweep the seas.

To a Solemn Musick

Is "merchant" an inglorious name?
  No; fit for Pindar such a theme;
Too great for me; I pant beneath the weight.
  If loud as Ocean were my voice,
  If words and thoughts to court my choice
Outnumber'd sands, I could not reach its height.

  Merchants o'er proudest heroes reign;
  Those trade in blessing, these in pain,
At slaughter swell, and shout while nations groan.
  With purple monarchs merchants vie;
  If great to spend, what to supply?
Priests pray for blessings; merchants pour them down.

  Kings, merchants are in league and love,
  Earth's odours pay soft airs above,
That o'er the teeming field prolific range.
  Planets are merchants; take, return,
  Lustre and heat; by traffic burn:
The whole creation is one vast Exchange. . . .

  Hast thou look'd round the spacious earth?
  From Commerce, Grandeur's humble birth:
To GEORGE from Noah, empires living, dead,
  Their pride, their shame, their rise, their fall,—
  Time's whole plain chronicle is all
One bright encomium, undesign'd, on Trade!

                        IMPERIUM PELAGI.

Final Pæan

THEE, Trade! I first—who boast no store,
  Who owe thee nought—thus snatch from shore,
The shore of Prose, where thou hast slumbered long;
  And send thy flag triumphant down
  The tide of time to sure renown.
O bless my country! and thou pay'st my song. . . .

Not Pindar's theme with mine compares,
   As far surpassed as useful cares
Transcend diversion light and glory vain:
   The wreath fantastic, shouting throng,
   And panting steed to him belong,—
The charioteer's, not Empire's golden, reign. . . .

Be dumb, ye grovelling sons of verse,
   Who *sing* not actions, but *rehearse*,
And fool the Muse with impotent desire!
   Ye sacrilegious, who presume
   To tarnish Britain's naval bloom!
Sing Britain's fame with all her hero's fire.

The Chorus

Ye Sirens, sing; ye Tritons, blow;
   Ye Nereids, dance; ye billows, flow;
Roll to my measures, O ye starry throng!
   Ye winds, in concert breathe around;
   Ye navies, to the concert bound
From pole to pole; to Britain all belong;
Britain to Heaven; from Heaven descends my song.
                        IBID.

Ye Nations, Tremble! Parliament has Met

FROWN you?   Frown on; your hour is past!
   The signal wafted in that blast
Speaks Britain's awful Senate met; beware
   Lest in her scale (the womb of right!)
   With all your arms, you're found too light,
Till smiles increase that weight your frowns impair.

For, mark the scene of deep debate,
   Where Britons sit on Europe's fate;

What loom'd exploit adorns it and inspires?
 The walls, the very walls advise,
 Each mean, degenerate thought chastise,
And rouse the sons with all their fathers' fires;

Teach them the style they used of old.
 Would Britain have her anger told?
Oh, never let a meaner language sound
 Than that which through black ether rolls,
 Than that which prostrates human souls,
And rocks pale realms, when angry gods have frown'd!

Gods, and their noblest offspring here,
 Soft terms refused, impose severe:
Ye nations know! know, all ye sceptred powers!
 In sulphurous night, and massy balls,
 And floods of flame, the tempest falls,
When Pride presumes, and Britain's Senate lours.

A brighter era is begun;
 Our fame advances with the sun;
A virgin Senate blooms: her bosom heaves
 With something great, with something new;
 Something our god-like sires may view,
And not abash'd shrink back into their graves.

THE FOREIGN ADDRESS.

With a Yo, Ho, Ho [1]

O COULD I sing as you have fought,
 I'd raise a monument of thought,
Bright as the sun!—How you burn at my heart!
 How the drums all around
 Soul-rousing resound!

[1] *The Foreign Address* (1734) was written "in the Character of a Sailor."

Swift drawn from the thigh
How the swords flame on high!
How the cannon, deep knell,
Fates of kingdoms foretell!
How to battle, to battle, sick of feminine art,
How to battle, to conquest, to glory, we dart!

IBID.

La Pudeur Française

O BRITAIN, infamous for suicide!
An island in thy manners! far disjoin'd
From the whole world of rationals beside!
In ambient waves plunge thy polluted head,
Wash the dire stain, nor shock the Continent!

NIGHT THOUGHTS, NIGHT V.

JOHN DYER (1700–58)

THE REV. JOHN DYER left Westminster School to study art under Jonathan Richardson, turned from art to the Established Church, held two livings in Lincolnshire, composed *The Fleece, a Poem*, in 1757, and died in the following year of "a consumptive Disorder." Dr. Johnson came heavily down on *The Fleece*. "The subject, Sir, cannot be made poetical. How can a man write poetically of serges and druggets?"

The charge is not generally tenable. Vergil wrote poetically of sheep-scab and manure; and Dyer's image of the ram gladly resigning his fleecy tail to Lincoln and Bennett is poetic enough. Like one or two other poets of his age, he is puzzled by the insensibility of the Untaught Native to the blessings of Big Business; and his luscious description of the County Workhouse makes it seem almost sinful to be a pauper. Observe also, in the lines on Leeds, that Dyer is indifferent to smoke-abatement, and compare with his admiring approval of Business Men (continued through two books) the later disillusions of Cowper:

> "Merchants, unimpeachable of sin
> Against the charities of domestic life,
> Incorporated, seem at once to lose
> Their nature; and disclaiming all regard
> For mercy and the common rights of man,
> Build factories with blood, conducting trade
> At the sword's point, and dyeing the white robe
> Of innocent Commercial Justice red."

Pastoral

I

IN cold stiff soils the bleaters oft complain
Of gouty ails, by shepherds termed the halt:

76

Robert Browning, taking tea with the Browning Society

Those let the neighbouring fold or ready crook
Detain: and pour into their cloven feet
Corrosive drugs, deep-searching arsenic,
Dry alum, verdigris, or vitriol keen.
But if the doubtful mischief scarce appears,
'Twill serve to shift them to a drier turf,
And salt again: th' utility of salt
Teach thy slow swains: redundant humours cold
Are the diseases of the bleating kind.

THE FLEECE, BK. I.

II

Wild rove the flocks, no burdening fleece they bear,
In fervid climes: Nature gives naught in vain.
Carmenian wool on the broad tail alone
Resplendent swells, enormous in its growth:
As the sleek ram from green to green removes,
On aiding wheels his heavy pride he draws,
And glad resigns it to the hatter's use.

IBID., BK. II.

The Insensible Hottentot

MON'MOTAPA's coast
Is seldom visited; and the rough shore
Of Caffres, land of savage Hottentots,
Whose hands unnatural hasten to the grave
Their aged parents: what barbarity
And brutal ignorance, where social trade
Is held contemptible!

IBID., BK. IV.

The House Beautiful

Ho, ye poor, who seek,
Among the dwellings of the diligent,
For sustenance unearned; who stroll abroad
From house to house, with mischievous intent,
Feigning misfortune: Ho, ye lame, ye blind;
Ye languid limbs, with real want oppressed,
Who tread the rough highways, and mountains wild,
Through storms, and rains, and bitterness of heart;
Ye children of affliction, be compelled
To happiness: the long-wished daylight dawns,
When charitable rigour shall detain
Your step-bruis'd feet.   Even now the sons of trade,
Where'er the cultivated hamlets smile,
Erect the mansion [1]: here soft fleeces shine;
The card awaits you, and the comb, and wheel;
Here shroud you from the thunder of the storm;
No rain shall wet your pillow; here abounds
Pure beverage; here your viands are prepared;
To heal each sickness the physician waits,
And priest entreats to give your Maker praise.

Ibid., Bk. III.

Leeds for Pleasure

Wide around
Hillock and valley, farm and village, smile:
And ruddy roofs and chimney-tops appear,
Of busy Leeds, up-wafting to the clouds
The incense of thanksgiving: all is joy;
And trade and business guide the living scene. . . .
Lo, in throngs,
For every realm, the careful factors meet,

[1] This alludes to the Workhouses at Bristol, Birmingham, etc.—Author's Note.

Whispering each other.   In long ranks the bales,
Like war's bright files, beyond the sight extend.
Straight, ere the sounding bell the signal strikes,
Which ends the hour of traffic, they conclude
The speedy compact; and, well-pleas'd, transfer,
With mutual benefit, superior wealth
To many a kingdom's rent, or tyrant's hoard.

IBID.

WILLIAM SHENSTONE (1714–63)

SHENSTONE, whom Horace Walpole unkindly called "the water-gruel poet," was contemporary with Johnson at Pembroke College, Oxford; a large stout heavy man, reserved in manner and negligent in dress. His best verse is in *The Schoolmistress* (1742), which was praised by Johnson and Goldsmith; but Mr. Shenstone's real life-work was gardening, and he nearly ruined himself by improving an estate left him in 1745. A French admirer celebrated his labours in the following inscription, placed in the gardens of Ermenonville:

> "This plain stone
> To William Shenstone.
> In his writings he display'd
> A mind natural;
> At Leasowes he laid
> Arcadian greens rural."

The shepherd's lament for the Woollen Manufactory has moments of poetry; there are even more in the moving tale of Jessy, guileless daughter of the plain, towards whose ruin expense is no object, who is chased first by the robust poet, then by the birds and lambs, and who ends in such a damp and melancholy posture.

Home Industries First

The Song of Colin, a Discerning Shepherd, lamenting the State of the Woollen Manufactory.

"ADIEU, my flocks!" he said, "my wonted care,
  By sunny mountains, or by verdant shore;
May some more happy hand your fold prepare,
  And may you need your Colin's crook no more! . . .

"Ah! what avails the timorous lambs to guard,
  Though nightly cares with daily labours join,
If foreign sloth obtain the rich reward,
  If Gallia's craft the ponderous fleece purloin? . . .

"Ah! heedless Albion! too benignly prone
  Thy blood to lavish, and thy wealth resign!
Shall every other virtue grace thy throne,
  But quick-eyed Prudence never yet be thine?

"From the fair natives of this peerless hill
  Thou gav'st the sheep that browse Iberian plains;
Their plaintive cries the faithless region fill,
  Their fleece adorns a haughty foe's domains.

"Ill-fated flocks! from cliff to cliff they stray;
  Far from their dams, their native guardians far!
Where the soft shepherd, all the livelong day,
  Chaunts his proud mistress to the hoarse guitar.

"But Albion's youth her native fleece despise;
  Unmoved they hear the pining shepherd's moan;
In silky folds each nervous limb disguise,
  Allured by every treasure but their own.

"Oft have I hurried down the rocky steep,
  Anxious to see the wintry tempest drive;
Preserve, said I, preserve your fleece, my sheep!
  Ere long will Phyllis, will my love, arrive.

"Ere long she came: ah! woe is me! she came,
  Robed in the Gallic loom's extraneous twine;
For gifts like this they give their spotless fame,
  Resign their bloom, their innocence resign.

"Will no bright maid, by worth, by titles known,
  Give the rich growth of Britain's hills to Fame?
And let her charms, and her example, own
  That Virtue's dress and Beauty's are the same?

"Will no famed chief support this generous maid?
  Once more the patriot's arduous path resume?
And, comely from his native plains array'd,
  Speak future glory to the British loom?"

ELEGY XVIII.

Goats and Botanists

AND see Plinlimmon! even the youthful sight
  Scales the proud hill's ethereal cliffs with pain!
Such, Caer-Caradoc! thy stupendous height,
  Whose ample shade obscures th' Iernian main.

Bleak, joyless regions! where, by science fired,
  Some prying sage his lonely step may bend;
There, by the love of novel plants inspired,
  Invidious view the clambering goats ascend.

ELEGY XXI.

The Chase of Jessy

*Elegy, Describing the Sorrow of an Ingenuous Mind on the
Melancholy Event of a Licentious Amour*

OF folly studious, even of vices vain,
  Ah, vices gilded by the rich and gay!
I chased the guileless daughters of the plain,
  Nor dropp'd the chase till Jessy was my prey.

Poor artless maid! to stain thy spotless name,
  Expense, and Art, and Toil united strove;
To lure a breast that felt the purest flame,
  Sustain'd by Virtue, but betray'd by Love. . . .

Nine envious moons matured her growing shame,
  Erewhile to flaunt it in the face of day,
When scorn'd of Virtue, stigmatised by Fame,
  Low at my feet desponding Jessy lay.

"Henry," she said, "by thy dear form subdued,
  See the sad relics of a nymph undone!
I find, I find this rising sob renew'd;
  I sigh in shades, and sicken at the sun. . . .

"The vocal birds that raise their matin strain,
  The sportive lambs, increase my pensive moan;
All seem to chase me from the cheerful plain,
  And talk of truth and innocence alone.

"If through the garden's flowery tribes I stray,
  Where bloom the jasmines that could once allure,
'Hope not to find delight in us,' they say,
  'For we are spotless, Jessy; we are pure.' . . .

"Now the grave old alarm the gentler young,
  And all my fame's abhorr'd contagion flee;
Trembles each lip, and falters every tongue,
  That bids the morn propitious smile on me.[1] . . .

"Raise me from earth; the pains of want remove,
  And let me, silent, seek some friendly shore;
There only, banish'd from the form I love,
  My weeping virtue shall relapse no more. . . .

"Force not my tongue to ask its scanty bread,
  Nor hurl thy Jessy to the vulgar crew;
Not such the parent's board at which I fed!
  Not such the precepts from his lips I drew."

[1] i.e. That says good morning to me.

She spoke—nor was I born of savage race,
    Nor could these hands a niggard boon assign;
Grateful she clasp'd me in a last embrace,
    And vow'd to waste her life in prayers for mine.

I saw her foot the lofty bark ascend,
    I saw her breast with every passion heave;
I left her—torn from every earthly friend;
    Oh, my hard bosom! which could bear to leave.

Brief let me be: the fatal storm arose;
    The billows raged, the pilot's art was vain;
O'er the tall mast the circling surges close;
    My Jessy—floats upon the watery plain!

And—see my youth's impetuous fires decay:
    Seek not to stop Reflection's bitter tear;
But warn the frolic, and instruct the gay,
    From Jessy floating on her watery bier.

ELEGY XXVI.

JOSEPH WARTON (1722–1800)

Of the Rev. Joseph Warton it is written in Chalmers's *Life*: "Having left the University after a short residence, he mixed early with the world, sought and enjoyed the society of the fair sex, and tempered his studious habits with the tender and polite attentions necessary in promiscuous intercourse."

Promiscuity and studiousness notwithstanding, Mr. Warton found time to publish in 1746, while a curate at Basingstoke, seventeen *Odes on Various Subjects*, favourably compared by the critics with Collins's. In April 1751 we find the amiable clergyman in France with the Duke of Bolton, his patron, and the Duke's mistress, Lavinia Fenton, the captivating Polly of *The Beggar's Opera*; all three with equal eagerness awaiting news of the Duchess's death, for his Grace had promised Mr. Warton a comfortable benefice for performing the marriage ceremony. The Duchess, however, stuck to her living and so deprived the clergyman of his, and in September Mr. Warton returned to England. In 1753 he published his *Vergil*, in four volumes octavo, and in 1755, despairing of preferment, turned to a scholastic career and became headmaster of Winchester in 1766. He afterwards retired elsewhere in Hampshire, with two cosy livings.

Mr. Warton, a persevering poet but a sagacious critic, is familiar to every reader of Boswell. He was, says Fanny Burney, a voluble talker, and would hug his auditor in the excitement of argument. Johnson loved him, but not invariably. For such a sociable soul the exercise in the dismals which follows must have meant a severe effort.

Le Spleen

Farewell, thou dimpled cherub, Joy,
Thou rose-crown'd ever-smiling boy,
Wont thy sister Hope to lead,
To dance along the primrose mead!

No more, bereft of happy hours,
I seek your lute-resounding bow'rs,
But to yon ruin'd tow'r repair,
To meet the god of groans, Despair;
Who, on that ivy-darken'd ground,
Still takes at eve his silent round,
Or sits yon new-made grave beside,
Where lies a frantic suicide:
While lab'ring sighs my heart-strings break,
Thus to the sullen power I speak:
   "Haste with thy poison'd dagger, haste,
To pierce this sorrow-laden breast!
Or lead me, at the dead of night,
To some sea-beat mountain's height,
Whence with headlong haste I'll leap
To the dark bosom of the deep;
Or show me, far from human eye,
Some cave to muse in, starve, and die;
No weeping friend or brother near,
My last, fond, falt'ring words to hear!"

ODE AGAINST DESPAIR.

JAMES GRAINGER (1721–67)

JAMES GRAINGER, M.D., is yet another of the eighteenth-century practitioners in viscera and verse. After serving as a doctor in Pulteney's Regiment he settled in London, came in contact with the Johnsonian circle, wrote, published, and in 1759 went out to Jamaica, where he died of West Indian fever. His principal works are: *An Obstinate Case of Dysentery Cured by Lime-Water*, *A Poetical Translation of the Elegies of Tibullus*, and (1759) *The Sugar-Cane, a Poem*, which Johnson reviewed in the *London Chronicle*. Johnson, who thought Grainger an agreeable and benevolent man, did not care for the poem. "What could he make of a sugar-cane?" he said to Boswell. "One might as well write *The Parsley-Bed, a Poem*, or *The Cabbage Garden, a Poem*." And Boswell reports the explosion of mirth which greeted the reading aloud at Reynolds's house of the apostrophe:

> "Now, Muse, let's sing of rats,"

with which the poet had pompously begun a fresh paragraph.

The West Indian ballad of *Bryan and Pereene*, with its affecting parting not only of the lovers but of the lover himself, is pretty enough. The extracts from *The Sugar-Cane* have perhaps more substance. Grainger's violent attack on French sugar-manipulators will surprise and charm all who have hitherto turned with loathing from the English Grocer, of whom it is written:

> "He sells us sands of Araby
> As sugar for cash down"—

the more so because Grainger awards him, by implication, a halo of the largest size. The verses beginning "And pity the poor planter" lull the reader into a drowsy security from which the last line blasts him with something of the effect of a trench-mortar, and the poet's bland counsel to slave-owners desirous of profit is entirely at one with the sentiments of the pious citizens of Bristol, who made such fortunes in the trade.

Bryan and Pereene

THE north-west wind did briskly blow,
  The ship was safely moor'd,
Young Bryan thought the boat's crew slow,
  And so leap'd over board.

Pereene, the pride of Indian dames,
  His heart did long enthral;
And whoso his impatience blames,
  I wot ne'er lov'd at all.

A long, long year, one month and day,
  He dwelt on English land,
Nor once in thought would ever stray,
  Though ladies sought his hand.

For Bryan he was tall and strong,
  Right blithesome roll'd his een,
Sweet was his voice whene'er he sang,
  He scant had twenty seen.

But who the countless charms can draw,
  That grac'd his mistress true?
Such charms the old world never saw,
  Nor oft I ween the new.

Her raven hair plays round her neck,
  Like tendrils of the vine;
Her cheek red dewy rose-buds deck,
  Her eyes like diamonds shine.

Soon as his well-known ship she spied,
  She cast her weeds away,
And to the palmy shore she hied,
  All in her best array.

In sea-green silk so neatly clad,
  She there impatient stood;
The crew with wonder saw the lad
  Repel the foaming flood.

Her hands a handkerchief display'd,
  Which he at parting gave;
Well pleas'd, the token he survey'd,
  And manlier beat the wave.

Her fair companions one and all
  Rejoicing crowd the strand;
For now her lover swam in call,
  And almost touch'd the land.

Then through the white surf did she haste
  To clasp her lovely swain;
When, ah! a shark bit through his waist;
  His heart's blood dy'd the main!

He shriek'd! his half sprung from the wave,
  Streaming with purple gore,
And soon it found a living grave,
  And, ah! was seen no more.

Now haste, now haste, ye maids, I pray,
  Fetch water from the spring:
She falls, she falls, she dies away,
  And soon her knell they ring.

Now each May morning round her tomb,
  Ye fair, fresh flow'rets strew,
So may your lovers 'scape his doom,
  Her hapless fate 'scape you.

Crescendo

AND pity the poor planter, when the blast,
Fell plague of Heaven! perdition of the isles!
Attacks his waving gold.   Though well-manur'd;
A richness though thy fields from Nature boast;
Though seasons pour; this pestilence invades:
Too oft it seizes the glad infant throng,
Nor pities their green nonage: their broad blades,
Of which the graceful wood-nymphs erst compos'd
The greenest garlands to adorn their brows,
First pallid, sickly, dry, and wither'd show;
Unseemly stains succeed; which, nearer view'd
By microscopic arts, small eggs appear,
Dire fraught with reptile life; alas, too soon
They burst their filmy gaol, and crawl abroad,
Bugs of uncommon shape.

THE SUGAR-CANE, BK. II.

The Shame of France

FALSE Gallia's sons, that hoe the ocean isles,
Mix with their sugar loads of worthless sand,
Fraudful, their weight of sugar to increase.
Far be such guile from Britain's honest swains.
Such arts, awhile, th' unwary may surprise,
And benefit th' impostor; but, ere long,
The skilful buyer will the fraud detect,
And, with abhorrence, reprobate the name.

IBID., BK. III.

Advice to Slave-Owners

I

MUST thou from Afric reinforce thy gang?—
Let health and youth their every sinew firm;
Clear roll their ample eye; their tongue be red;
Broad swell their chest; their shoulders wide expand;

Not prominent their belly; clean and strong
Their thighs and legs, in just proportion rise.
Such soon will brave the fervours of the clime;
And free from ails, that kill thy Negro-train,
An useful servitude will long support.

II

Worms lurk in all: yet, pronest they to worms,
Who from Mundingo sail. When therefore such
Thou buy'st, for sturdy and laborious they,
Straight let some learned leech strong med'cines give,
Till food and climate both familiar grow.

III

One precept more, it much imports to know.
The Blacks, who drink the Quanza's lucid stream,
Fed by ten thousand streams, are prone to bloat,
Whether at home or in these ocean isles:
And though nice art the water may subdue,
Yet many die; and few, for many a year,
Just strength attain to labour for their lord.
   Wouldst thou secure thine Ethiop from these ails,
Which change of climate, change of waters breed,
And food unusual? let Machaon draw
From each some blood, as age and sex require.

IBID.

Call to the Muse

OF composts shall the Muse disdain to sing?
Nor soil her heavenly plumes? The sacred Muse
Nought sordid deems, but what is base; nought fair,
Unless true Virtue stamp it with her seal.
Then, planter, wouldst thou double thine estate,
Never, ah! never, be asham'd to tread
Thy dung-heaps.

IBID.

THOMAS WARTON, THE YOUNGER
(1728–90)

THOMAS WARTON the Younger was a Don of Trinity, Oxford, whose eccentricities gave his brother Dons enduring pain; for he was a fat little husky cheerful red-faced man who loved beer, tobacco, taverns, and low company, and had (as might be expected) the oddest passion for "the Gothick." Like his brother Joseph he was one of the Johnsonian circle, though he and the Sage did not invariably enjoy each other's company. He so far complied with fashion as to compose (1745) *The Pleasures of Melancholy*, but it could be plainly seen that he was distorting his features with difficulty. His *Triumph of Isis* (1749), an heroic poem in praise of his University, was very popular. He published later an anthology of Oxford wit. His *Observations on the "Faery Queen" of Spenser* made his reputation as a critic, which was increased (at home, but not abroad) by his *Theocritus*. He became Professor of Poetry at Oxford in 1757 and Poet Laureate in 1785, as may be gathered from his address to Queen Charlotte, following. Compare, with his hymning of Property, Dyer's praise of Liberty,

> "whose hand benign
> Teaches unwearied Toil to clothe the fields,
> And on his various fruits inscribes the name
> Of Property."

Of George, and Property

Lo! this the land, where Freedom's sacred rage
Has glow'd untamed through many a martial age. . . .
Here wak'd the flame, that still superior braves
The proudest threats of Gaul's ambitious slaves;

Here Chivalry, stern school of valour old,
Her noblest feats of knightly fame enroll'd;
Heroic champions caught the clarion's call,
And throng'd the feast in Edward's banner'd hall;
While chiefs, like GEORGE, approv'd in worth alone,
Unlock'd chaste Beauty's adamantine zone.
Lo! the famed isle, which hails thy chosen sway,
What fertile fields her temperate suns display!
Where Property secures the conscious swain,
And guards, while Plenty gives, the golden grain.

ON THE MARRIAGE OF THE KING.

EDWARD JERNINGHAM (1727–1812)

THERE have been better English poets than EDWARD JER-
NINGHAM; there has been none more polite. Fanny Burney,
with her unerring eye, describes Mr. Jerningham in her diary
as "a mighty delicate gentleman, all daintification in manner,
speech, and dress." He belonged to that notable Norfolk
Catholic family the Jerninghams of Costessey, and was
educated, like most contemporary Catholics of his rank,
at Douai and Paris; but after returning to England and wit-
nessing the coronation of George III Mr. Jerningham decided
to discard the faith of his ancestors—a decision which was
socially, indeed, of some benefit, for that faith was practised
in England in his day for the most part by obscure persons of
no condition and the Penal Laws were still in force. He was
rewarded by the approval and friendship of men of the highest
quality, Lord Chesterfield, Lord Harcourt, Lord Carlisle,
Horace Walpole; an approval in no way lessened by Mr. Jerningham's toying, in an urbane way, with letters. He wrote
a great deal. He wrote many elegies and some plays, and his
tragedy *The Siege of Berwick* ran for five nights at Covent
Garden. He also wrote on Scandinavian Poetry and on the
Alexandrian School, and translated from M. Bossuet.

The delicacy of Mr. Jerningham, something of a Henry
James character, is amply discovered in the poem *Il Latte*,
which follows, whose title (in English, "Milk") stamps the
piece with its dominant note, that exquisite *pudeur* which the
Continent so hopelessly envies and admires. With her face
thus veiled in the decent obscurity of a foreign language the
Muse can proceed with elegance to treat of physiological facts
otherwise impossibly crude. Seldom has the feminine bosom
been celebrated, seldom have wet-nurses been denounced
(Stanza 7) with such gentlemanly decorum, and seldom has
the performance of an infant's taking nourishment at the
natural source been so fastidiously and at the same time so
poetically described as in our last stanza.

94

There are actually eleven more, singing the social, literary, and political triumphs awaiting the maternal breast-fed. We stop at the summit.

Il Latte

Ye fair, for whom the hands of Hymen weave
  The nuptial wreath to deck your virgin brow,
With pleasing pains the conscious bosom heave,
  And on the kindling cheek the blushes glow: . . .

To you I sing.—Ah! ere the raptur'd youth
  With trembling hand removes the jealous veil,
Where, long regardless of the vows of truth,
  Unsocial coyness stamp'd th' ungrateful seal:

Allow the poet round your flowing hair,
  Cull'd from an humble vale, a wreath to twine,
To Beauty's altar with the Loves repair,
  And wake the lute beside that living shrine:

That sacred shrine! where female virtue glows,
  To which retreat the warm affections fly;
Where Love is born, where strong attachment grows,
  Where frames pure Constancy the faithful tie:

That shrine! where Nature with presaging aim,
  What time her friendly aid Lucina brings,
The snowy nectar pours, delightful stream!
  Where flutt'ring Cupids dip their purple wings:

Say why, illustrious daughters of the Great,
  Lives not the nursling at your tender breast?
By you protected in his frail estate?
  By you attended, and by you caress'd?

To venal hands, alas! can you resign
　　The Parent's task, the Mother's pleasing care?
To venal hands the smiling babe consign?
　　While Hymen starts, and Nature drops a tear.

When 'mid the polish'd circle ye rejoice,
　　Or roving join fantastic Pleasure's train,
Unheard perchance the nursling lifts his voice,
　　His tears unnotic'd, and unsooth'd his pain.

Ah! what avails the coral crown'd with gold?
　　In heedless infancy the title vain?
The colours gay the purfled scarfs unfold?
　　The splendid nurs'ry, and th' attendant train? . . .

Nor wonder, should Hygeia, blissful Queen!
　　Her wonted salutary gifts recall,
While haggard Pain applies his dagger keen;
　　And o'er the cradle Death unfolds his pall. . . .

For you, ye plighted fair, when Hymen crowns
　　With tender offspring your unshaken love,
Behold them not with Rigour's chilling frowns,
　　Nor from your sight unfeelingly remove.

Unsway'd by Fashion's dull unseemly jest,
　　Still to the bosom let your infant cling,
There banquet oft, an ever-welcome guest,
　　Unblam'd inebriate at that healthful spring.

CHRISTOPHER SMART (1722–71)

OF CHRISTOPHER SMART, sometime Fellow of Pembroke College, Cambridge, it may be said broadly that he was fond of taverns and the poet Gray. In 1751 mental disorders took him to Bedlam, where his addiction to prayer without ceasing left no doubt in the minds of several doctors and clergymen that he was very mad indeed. His wretched life was spent in poverty, drink, and hacking for booksellers in Grub Street; his finest poem, the *Song to David*, was written partly with charcoal on the walls and partly with a key on the panels of his cell in Bedlam in 1763. He died in the Rules of the King's Bench.

The first extract following is a dogged but not unagreeable Georgic, the second will appeal (in the modern phrase) to every housewife.

Hops and Props

WHEN Phœbus looks through Aries on the spring,
And vernal flow'rs teem with the dulcet fruit,
Autumnal pride! delay not then thy sets
In Tellus' facile bosom to depose
Timely; if thou art wise the bulkiest choose;
To every root three joints indulge, and form
The quincunx with well-regulated hills.
Soon from the dung-enrichèd earth, their heads
The young plants will uplift, their virgin arms
They'll stretch, and, marriageable, claim the pole. . . .
But yet in the novitiate of their love,
And tenderness of youth, suffice small shoots
Cut from the widow'd willow, nor provide

Poles unsurmountable as yet.   'Tis then,
When twice bright Phœbus' vivifying ray,
Twice the cold touch of Winter's icy hand,
They've felt; 'tis then we fell sublimer props.

THE HOP-GARDEN, BK. I.

The Nail in the Grass

WHEN in the bag thy hops the rustic treads,
Let him wear heelless sandals; nor presume
Their fragrancy barefooted to defile:
Such filthy ways for slaves in Malaga
Leave we to practise—whence I've often seen,
When beautiful Dorinda's iv'ry hand
Has built the pastry fabric (food divine
For Christmas gambols, and the hour of mirth),
As the dried foreign fruit, with piercing eye,
She culls suspicious—lo! she starts, she frowns
With indignation at the Negro's nail.

IBID., BK. II.

OLIVER GOLDSMITH (1728–74)

THE Muse of OLIVER GOLDSMITH is perceived at her most girlish in the ensuing selection from *The Captivity*, a poetic drama which has much in common with the libretto of *Les Cloches de Corneville*, with its artless choruses:

> "*Voyez par ci,*
> *Voyez par là,*
> *Comment trouvez-vous cela ?*"

95548

Had she consistently kept this level perhaps Goldsmith would not have died owing two thousand pounds ("Was ever poet," said Johnson, holding up his hands, "so trusted before?"), and Mr. Filby the tailor, at the sign of the Harrow in Water Lane, might have been paid for the famous bloom-coloured coat, the blue velvet, the silver-grey tamboured waistcoat, and other finery supplied to the Doctor's order. Goldsmith's library was rich in French literature, including the long-extinct plays of Brueys, La Chaussée, Dancourt, and Destouches, and many contemporary minor poets; to whom, no doubt, he owed something of his inspiration for *The Captivity*.

Observe, incidentally, the brisk and efficient conclusion of the Second Prophet's remark. As who should say, "Ay, ay, sir!"

Entry of the Villagers

First Priest

COME on, my companions, the triumph display,
  Let rapture the minutes employ;
The sun calls us out on this festival day,
  And our monarch partakes in the joy.

Second Priest

Like the sun, our great monarch all rapture supplies,
  Both similar blessings bestow;
The sun with his splendour illumines the skies,
  And our monarch enlivens below.

A Chaldean Woman

Haste, ye sprightly sons of pleasure,
Love presents the fairest treasure,
  Leave all other joys for me.

An Attendant

Say rather, Love's delights despising,
Haste to raptures ever rising,
  Wine shall bless the brave and free.

THE CAPTIVITY.

Cause and Effect

COEVAL with man
Our empire began,
And never shall fall,
Till ruin shakes all;
When ruin shakes all
Then shall Babylon fall.

IBID.

A Sombre Moment

First Prophet

FROM north, from south, from east, from west,
  Conspiring nations come;
Tremble, thou vice-polluted breast,
  Blasphemers, all be dumb.

The tempest gathers all around,
  On Babylon it lies,
Down with her!—down, down to the ground,
  She sinks, she groans, she dies.

Second Prophet

Down with her, Lord, to lick the dust,
  Ere yonder setting sun;
Serve her as she has served the just;
  'Tis fixed—it shall be done.

IBID.

JOHN DUNCOMBE (1729–86)

The Rev. John Duncombe, Fellow of Corpus Christi, Cambridge, married (1761) Susanna, daughter of Mr. Joseph Highmore, the artist. Miss Highmore's often - reproduced sketch of the Grotto at Fulham belonging to Mr. Richardson, the eminent novelist, includes among its figures that of the gifted clergyman to whom she had plighted her troth. The six figures—Miss Highmore, Mr. Mulso, Mr. Mulso the Younger, Miss Mulso (afterwards "the celebrated Mrs. Chapone"), Miss Prescott, and the Rev. Mr. Duncombe—sit grouped in attitudes of dignified attention to Mr. Richardson, who is reading aloud the MS. of *Sir Charles Grandison*, that delicious work. "The Rev. John Duncombe," observes Austin Dobson, "is taking snuff with an air which would do credit to the *vieille Cour*, or even to the irreproachable Sir Charles himself."

Mr. Duncombe, who held comfortable livings in Canterbury, where he died, was among the genteel contributors to the *World*. From the following extract from *The Feminead, or Female Genius* (1754), it may be perceived with what sincere zeal he can celebrate the virtues of a Peeress, in periods which only one poet since has been able faintly to recapture:

> "All hail to the vessel of Pecksniff the sire,
>   And favouring breezes to fan;
> While Tritons flock round it, and proudly admire
>   The architect, artist, and man!"

Females, Sacred and Profane

The modest Muse a veil with pity throws
O'er Vice's friends, and Virtue's female foes;
Abash'd she views the bold unblushing mien
Of modern Manley, Centlivre, and Behn;

And grieves to see one nobly born disgrace
Her modest sex, and her illustrious race.
Tho' harmony thro' all their numbers flow'd,
And genuine wit its every grace bestow'd,
Nor genuine wit, nor harmony, excuse
The dangerous sallies of a wanton Muse:
Nor can such tuneful, but immoral, lays
Expect the tribute of impartial praise:
As soon might PHILIPS, PILKINGTON, and VANE,
Deserv'd applause for spotless virtue gain.

But hark! what Nymph, in Frome's embroidered
  vale,
With strains seraphic swells the vernal gale?
With what sweet sounds the bordering forest rings?
For sportive Echo catches, as she sings,
Each falling accent, studious to prolong
The warbled notes of ROWE's ecstatic song.
Old Avon pleas'd his reedy forehead rears,
And polish'd ORRERY delighted hears.
See with what transport she resigns her breath,
Snatch'd by a sudden, but a wish'd-for death!
Releas'd from earth, with smiles she soars on high
Amidst her kindred spirits of the sky,
Where faith and love those endless joys bestow,
That warm'd her lays, and fill'd her hopes below.

Nor can her noble Friend escape unseen,
Or from the Muse her modest virtues screen;
How, sweetly blended, to our wondering eyes,
The peeress, poetess, and Christian rise:
And tho' the Nine her tuneful strains inspire,
We less her genius, than her heart, admire,
Pleas'd, 'midst the great, one truly good to see,
And proud to tell that SOMERSET is she.

By generous views one Peeress more demands
A grateful tribute from all female hands;
One, who to shield them from the worst of foes,
In their just cause dar'd Pope himself oppose.

Their own dark forms deceit and envy wear,
By IRWIN touch'd with Truth's celestial spear,
By her disarm'd, ye witlings! now give o'er
Your empty sneers, and shock the sex no more.

THE FEMINEAD.

ERASMUS DARWIN (1731–1802)

ERASMUS DARWIN, M.B., grandfather and to some extent precursor of the more famous Darwin whose evolutionary hypotheses were for some time accepted as law, was a Lichfield physician of some personality. His bodily and mental vigour was extreme, his eccentricities included that of drinking only "English wines," his temper was imperious and irascible, and he heartily disliked Dr. Johnson, who returned his dislike thoroughly: for each lion deemed the other a bore.

Darwin's grotesque verse, a critic has remarked, everywhere shows a powerful mind. *The Loves of the Plants* was published in 1789, and was followed by *Zoonomia, or Laws of Organic Life*, and *Phytologia, or the Philosophy of Agriculture and Gardening*. The first was praised by Cowper, Hayley, and Walpole; two of these being men of piety and benevolence, the third a man of fashion. The vivid romance of Eliza which follows is unique in that never before has an English (or any other) poet so clearly demonstrated the folly of taking the children to see a battle. Not only does the constant rushing about make them peevish, fretful, and overheated, but a ball may easily sink into their mother's neck and she may fall to the ground, hiding her babes within her blood-stained vest. The agony of the warrior after finishing the battle is graphically conveyed; yet he, too, has a blood-stained vest, in which he immediately wraps the children, thereby staving off the inevitable rash, whooping-cough, and croup.

It might be justly added that in this age of universal exploitation in print of erotic situations Darwin's tribute to the chastity of the Truffle strikes a welcome note. His respiring lampreys will probably arouse little emotion in a generation to whom similar embraces have become, by assiduous contemplation of American superfilms, a commonplace.

Eliza at the Battle

Now stood Eliza on the wood-crown'd height
O'er Minden's plains, spectatress of the fight;
Sought with bold eye amid the bloody strife
Her dearer self, the partner of her life;
From hill to hill the rushing host pursued,
And view'd his banner, or believed she view'd.
Pleased with the distant roar, with quicker tread,
Fast by his hand one lisping boy she led;
And one fair girl, amid the loud alarm,
Slept on her kerchief, cradled on her arm;
While round her brows bright beams of honour dart,
And love's warm eddies circle round her heart.
—Near and more near th' intrepid beauty press'd,
Saw through the driving smoke his dancing crest,
Heard the exulting shout—"They run!—They run!"
"He's safe!" she cried, "he's safe! the battle's won!"
—A ball now hisses through the airy tides
(Some Fury wings it, and some Demon guides),
Parts the fine locks her graceful head that deck,
Wounds her fair ear, and sinks into her neck;
The red stream issuing from her azure veins
Dyes her white veil, her ivory bosom stains.
—"Ah me!" she cried, and sinking on the ground,
Kiss'd her dear babes, regardless of the wound:
"Oh, cease not yet to beat, thou vital urn,
Wait, gushing life, oh! wait my love's return!"
Hoarse barks the wolf, the vulture screams from far,
The angel, Pity, shuns the walks of war;—
"Oh, spare, ye war-hounds, spare their tender age!
On me, on me," she cried, "exhaust your rage!"
Then with weak arms, her weeping babes caress'd,
And sighing, hid them in her blood-stain'd vest.

From tent to tent th' impatient warrior flies,
Fear in his heart, and frenzy in his eyes:

Eliza's name along the camp he calls,
Eliza echoes through the canvas walls;
Quick through the murmuring gloom his footsteps tread,
O'er groaning heaps, the dying and the dead,
Vault o'er the plain,—and in the tangled wood,—
Lo! dead Eliza—weltering in her blood!
Soon hears his listening son the welcome sounds,
With open arms and sparkling eyes he bounds:
"Speak low," he cries, and gives his little hand,
"Mamma's asleep upon the dew-cold sand;
Alas! we both with cold and hunger quake—
Why do you weep? Mamma will soon awake."
—"She'll wake no more!" the hopeless mourner cried,
Upturned his eyes, and clasp'd his hands, and sigh'd;
Stretch'd on the ground, awhile entranced he lay,
And press'd warm kisses on the lifeless clay;
And then upsprung with wild convulsive start,
And all the father kindled in his heart.
"Oh, Heaven!" he cried, "my first rash vow forgive!
These bind to earth, for these I pray to live."
Round his chill babes he wrapp'd his crimson vest,
And clasp'd them, sobbing, to his aching breast.

THE LOVES OF THE PLANTS.

Fine Figure of a Nymph

GIGANTIC Nymph! the fair KLEINHOVIA reigns,
The grace and terror of Orixia's plains.
O'er her warm cheek the blush of beauty swims,
And nerves Herculean bend her sinewy limbs;
With frolic eye she views the affrighted throng,
And shakes the meadows as she towers along;
With playful violence displays her charms,
And bears her trembling lover in her arms.

IBID.

"*Ae Fond Kiss, and Then——*"

So still the Tadpole cleaves the watery vale,
With balanc'd fins and undulating tail;
New lungs and limbs proclaim his second birth,
Breathe the dry air, and bound upon the earth.
Allied to fish, the Lizard cleaves the flood,
With one-cell'd heart, and dark frigescent blood;
Half-reasoning Beavers long-unbreathing dart
Through Eirie's waves with perforated heart;
With gills and lungs respiring Lampreys steer,
Kiss the rude rocks, and suck till they adhere; .
With gills pulmonic breathes th' enormous Whale,
And spouts aquatic columns to the gale.

THE TEMPLE OF NATURE.

The Maiden Truffle

So the lone Truffle, lodged beneath the earth,
Shoots from paternal roots the tuberous birth.
No stamen-males ascend, and breathe above,
No seed-born offspring lives by female love. . .
So the male Polypus parental swims,
And branching infants bristle all his limbs.
So the lone Tænia, as he grows, prolongs
His flatten'd form with young adherent throngs;
Unknown to sex the pregnant Oyster swells,
And coral-insects build their radiate shells.

IBID.

The Birth of KNO_3

HENCE orient Nitre owes its sparkling birth,
And with prismatic crystals gems the earth,
O'er tottering domes the filmy foliage crawls,
Or frosts with branching plumes the mould'ring walls;
As woos Azotic Gas the virgin Air,
And veils in crimson clouds the yielding fair.

THE ECONOMY OF VEGETATION.

Mr. Matthew Arnold
To him, Miss Mary Augusta, his niece: "Why, Uncle Matthew, oh,
why, will not you be always wholly serious?"

THOMAS CHATTERTON (1752–70)

OF CHATTERTON it is said that after the composition, at the age of ten, of an Ode on the Last Judgment he became more cheerful than he had formerly been. How he fed his eager mind on antique charters and documents ransacked from the muniment-room of St. Mary Redcliffe, Bristol; how he drew up for honest Mr. Burgum the pewterer a genealogical table proving his descent from the Norman knight de Bergham; how he astonished literary England and deceived such authorities as Warton and the President of the Society of Antiquaries with his Rowley forgeries and their medieval air; how he struggled almost successfully with his pen in London and died of a dose of arsenic in a dusky Holborn court at the age of eighteen, has been sufficiently told. His genius has been celebrated by more fortunate poets, Wordsworth, Byron, Scott, Shelley, Southey, Alfred de Vigny, Rossetti. The machinery of his Rowley Poems has been briskly described as "a factitious ancient diction, at once obsolete and heterogeneous"—as in *Ye Olde Elizabethanne Tea-Shope.*

Chatterton lacked to some extent a sense of humour, as the verses following may show. Compare, with the threnody on Mr. Smith, Dr. Watts on Mr. Gunston:

> "In the lonesome vault,
> Mindless of Watts and Friendship, cold he lies."

Mr. Baker is Well

O'ERWHELM'D with pleasure at the joyful news,
I strung the chorded shell, and woke the Muse.
Begin, O servant of the sacred Nine,
And echo joy through every nervous line;
Bring down th' ethereal choir to aid the song;
Let boundless rapture smoothly glide along.

My Baker's well!   Oh, words of sweet delight!
Now, now, my Muse, soar up th' Olympic height.
What wondrous numbers can the goddess find,
To paint th' ecstatic raptures of my mind?
I leave it to a goddess more divine,
The beauteous Hoyland shall employ my line.

TO A FRIEND.

Miss Hoyland is Coy

AH! Hoyland, empress of my heart,
When will thy breast admit the dart,
  And own a mutual flame?
When, wandering in the myrtle groves,
Shall mutual pleasures seal our loves—
  Pleasures without a name?

Thou greatest beauty of the sex,
When will the little god perplex
  The mansions of thy breast?
When wilt thou own a flame as pure
As that seraphic souls endure,
  And make thy Baker blest?

ODE TO MISS HOYLAND.

Mr. Smith is Dead

ASCEND, my Muse, on Sorrow's sable plume,
  Let the soft number meet the swelling sigh;
With laureated chaplets deck the tomb,
  The blood-stained tomb where Smith and comfort lie.

ELEGY ON MR. WILLIAM SMITH.

GEORGE CRABBE (1754–1832)

Love first moved George Crabbe to poetry in *Wheble's Magazine*, 1772, with a prize poem on *Hope*. A didactic poem entitled *Inebriety* followed, and a few years later Edmund Burke, who had become Crabbe's patron and had induced Dodsley to publish *The Library*, advised him to take orders in the Established Church as a more solid career. In 1782 Mr. Crabbe was appointed chaplain to the Duke of Rutland at Belvoir, and was thus enabled to marry his inspiration, Miss Elmy. In 1783 Johnson "revised" *The Village* for him, in the quaint fashion of the day. He was later given the living of Trowbridge in Wiltshire, and in 1819 published *Tales of the Hall*, a volume of verse which gave pleasure to—among many others—the great mind of Newman, who read it in youth and in old age and described it, in the language of the Schools, as "the accidental definition of a classic."

Crabbe's sturdy realism and contempt for *bergerie* gained him the friendship of Lord Holland, Scott, Campbell, and Moore, and the eulogies of Byron, Jane Austen, Wordsworth, FitzGerald, and Tennyson. He was a hearty, healthy clergyman, not altogether devoid of a sense of humour, with an eye for beauty in females. The extract following, which affords an interesting glimpse of the relaxation of a Business Man before the revue era, hints significantly enough of the preceding night's orgies. Together with the lines that succeed it, it might be satisfyingly defined in the words of the Sailor in *The Four Men*—"not sloppy verse, not wasty, pappy verse, not verse blanchified, but strong, heavy, brown, bad verse." It also marks the first (and last) appearance of the Clutterbuck in English Poetry.

A Business Man's Lair

Something one day occurr'd about a bill
That was not drawn with true mercantile skill,
And I was ask'd and authorised to go
To seek the firm of Clutterbuck and Co.;

Their hour was past—but when I urg'd the case,
There was a youth who named a second place,
Where, on occasions of important kind,
I might the man of occupation find,
In his retirement, where he found repose
From the vexations that in Business rose.

The house was good, but not so pure and clean
As I had houses of retirement seen;
Yet men, I knew, of meditation deep,
Love not their maidens should their studies sweep
His room I saw, and must acknowledge, there
Were not the signs of cleanliness or care:
A female servant, void of female grace,
Loose in attire, proceeded to the place;
She stared intrusive on my slender frame,
And boldly ask'd my business and my name.

I gave them both; and, left to be amused,
Well as I might, the parlour I perused. . . .
There were strange sights and scents about the room,
Of food high-season'd, and of strong perfume; . . .
A large old mirror, with once-gilded frame,
Reflected prints that I forbear to name—
Such as a youth might purchase—but, in truth,
Not a sedate or sober-minded youth.
The chairs in haste seem'd whirl'd about the room,
As when the sons of riot hurry home
And leave the troubled place to solitude and gloom.

TALES OF THE HALL: THE ELDER BROTHER.

The Baileys

The Squire, loq.:

"RICHARD," said he, "though I myself explore
With no distaste the annals of the poor,
And may with safety to a brother show
What of my humble friends I chance to know,
Richard, there are who call the subjects low.

"The host and hostess of the Fleece!—'tis base——
Would I could cast some glory round the place!

"The lively heroine once adorn'd a farm—
And William's virtue has a kind of charm;
Nor shall we, in our apprehension, need
Riches or rank——   I think we may proceed:
Virtue and worth there are who will not see
In humble dress, but low they cannot be."

IBID.: WILLIAM BAILEY.

A Bright Morning

THE morning shone in cloudless beauty bright;
Richard his letters read with much delight;
George from his pillow rose in happy tone,
His bosom's lord sat lightly on his throne:
They read the morning's news—they saw the sky
Inviting call'd them;—and the earth was dry.

IBID.: THE SISTERS.

Invitation to the Waltz

The Squire, loq.:

"BROTHER, there dwell, yon northern hill below,
Two favourite maidens, whom 'tis good to know,
Young, but experienced; dwellers in a cot,
Where they sustain and dignify their lot,
The best good girls in all our world below——
O! you must know them.—Come! and you shall know."

IBID.

ROBERT BURNS (1759–96)

THOUGH the genius of ROBERT BURNS is but grudgingly admitted by his countrymen, whose passion for their national poets Dunbar and James I tends perhaps to blind them to his undoubted merits, it must be allowed that Burns was a poet far above the average, a keen Freemason, a delightful table-companion, and a father whose habit of christening his daughters, legitimate or otherwise, by the name of Elizabeth shows some appreciation of official or Whig history.

The verses which follow are of his youth, but form part of the Collected Works. A modern critic has well observed that when Burns unwisely discards the vernacular his efforts resemble "nothing so much as a bather whose clothes have been stolen."

Verses

On the Death of Sir James Hunter Blair

THE lamp of day, with ill-presaging glare,
    Dim, cloudy, sunk beneath the western wave;
Th' inconstant blast howl'd thro' the darkening air,
    And hollow whistled in the rocky cave. . . .

Th' increasing blast roar'd round the beetling rocks,
    The clouds, swift-wing'd, flew o'er the starry sky;
The groaning trees untimely shed their locks,
    And shooting meteors caught the startled eye.

The paly moon rose in the livid east,
    And 'mong the cliffs disclos'd a stately form,
In weeds of woe, that frantic beat her breast,
    And mix'd her wailings with the raving storm.

Wild to my heart the filial pulses glow,
  'Twas Caledonia's trophied shield I view'd:
Her form majestic droop'd in pensive woe,
  The lightning of her eye in tears imbued. . .

"My patriot son fills an untimely grave!"
  With accents wild and lifted arm she cried;
"Low lies the hand that oft was stretch'd to save,
  Low lies the heart that swell'd with honest pride!

"A weeping country joins a widow's tear,
  The helpless poor mix with the orphan's cry;
The drooping Arts surround their patron's bier,
  And grateful Science heaves the heartfelt sigh. . . .

"My patriot falls—but shall he lie unsung,
  While empty greatness saves a worthless name?
No, every Muse shall join her tuneful tongue,
  And future ages hear his growing fame.

"And I will join a mother's tender cares,
  Through future times to make his virtues last,
That distant years may boast of other Blairs,"—
  She said, and vanish'd with the sweeping blast.

ROBERT MERRY ("DELLA CRUSCA")

(1755-98)

THE personality of ROBERT MERRY could have served
Barbey d'Aurevilley for an illustration of his thesis that
the torment of English puritanism is directly productive
not only of such revolt as the dandyism of Brummell
but less subtle forms of English eccentricity also. Merry
(Harrow and Cambridge) held a commission in the Horse
Guards during part of the American War, ruined himself at
high play, sold out at the age of twenty-two, travelled abroad,[1]
came to rest finally at Florence among the English colony
(then, as now, composed of exiles from choice and others on
account of the Police), plunged into poetry, contributed with
Mrs. Piozzi and others to the *Florence Miscellany*, became an
honorary member of the celebrated Della Cruscan Academy,
pursued such an openly-advertised intrigue with the Countess
Cowper that he had to leave Florence, returned to London,
and in June 1787 published in the *World*, over the signature
"Della Crusca," the opening blast of the fantasia with which
his name is associated. A passionate flirtation with Mrs. Cowley ("Anna Matilda") in the columns of the *World* followed,
until on July 14, 1789, the fall of the Bastille suddenly
altered Merry's whole existence. The French Revolution got
into his system, and henceforth nothing could bring him relief.

From now on he is—like that other English eccentric and
friend of Liberty who gratuitously hounded the unhappy
Dubarry to the guillotine *pour le bon motif*—the amateur
Jacobin. He composes *The Laurel of Liberty*, a poem, and
presents an address on free government to the Convention.
Having married the actress Elizabeth Brunton and taken her
to Paris, he is chased in 1792 by a mob of patriots who mistake

---

[1] To this period no doubt belongs the comic incident of the
Star and Garter Inn, Richmond, which Lamb wove into one of
the *Popular Fallacies*.

him for the Abbé Maury, and narrowly escapes. In 1793 he is in London again, emitting floods of oratory on his one topic and getting heavily into debt. In 1796 he goes with his wife to New York, where she makes a triumphal stage appearance, repeating her success in Philadelphia and other cities. In 1797 Merry publishes a drama in Philadelphia, and one catches a last glimpse of him in Baltimore in the next year, grown very fat and lethargic but still dogged as to the Revolution. He died of apoplexy soon afterwards.

His verse, which inspired a school of imitators, needs no comment except that it is difficult sometimes to believe that Mr. Merry, unlike his successors in Chelsea and in Paris, is not laughing heartily up his sleeve.

Elegy

Written after reading the "Sorrows of Werter"

ALAS, poor Werter! to himself a prey,
    The heart's excessive workings could not bear;
But sought his native heaven the nearest way,
    And fled from grief, from anguish, and despair.

The joys of prejudice he scorned to own,
    He pitied pride, and avarice, and power;
But oft on some rude rock at random thrown,
    He welcomed midnight's melancholy hour.

To view the moon's pale glimpse illume the wave,
    To list the sweeping blasts that sadly blow;
Down the rough steep, to hear the cat'racts rave;
    Such were the pleasures of this man of woe.

An isolated being here he stood,
    His strong sensations with how few could blend!
The wise, the great, the gay, perhaps the good,
    They knew him not—they could not comprehend.

Charlotte alone, by nature was designed
   To fill the vacuum of his generous breast;
He loved her beauty, he admired her mind;
   He lost that Charlotte, and he sought for rest!

The Rush to the Lakes

CANST thou, so keen of feeling! urge my fate,
And bid me mourn thee, yes, and mourn too late?
O rash severe decree! my madd'ning brain
Cannot the pond'rous agony sustain,
But forth I rush, as varying Frenzy leads,
To cavern'd lakes, or to the diamond meads,
O'er which the sultry moon-beams wide diffuse,
And slake their eager thirst with ling'ring dews;
Or to yon sullen slope that shuns the light,
Where the black forest weaves meridian night.
Disorder'd, lost, from hill to plain I run,
And with my mind's dark gloom obscure the sun.[1]

                    To ANNA MATILDA.

Some Terrify Lions

EAGER I'd traverse Lybia's plain,
The tawny lion's dread domain,
To meet thee there: nor flagging fear
Should ever on my cheek appear;
For e'en the forest's King obeys
Majestic Woman's potent gaze.

                    To ANNA MATILDA.

[1] As Henry Morley observes, "There was fog enough in his mind for that."

The Poet is Piqued

[On his Mistress's Momentary Refusal to open her Eyes]

CONJURE up demons from the main,
Storms upon storms indignant heap,
Bid Ocean howl, and Nature weep,
Till the Creator blush to see
How horrible his world can be:
While I will glory to blaspheme,
And make the joys of hell my theme.

To ANNA MATILDA.

The Tiff

"ILL-FATED BARD!" she cried, "whose lengthening grief
Had won the pathos of my lyre's relief,
For whom, full oft, I've loiter'd to rehearse
In phrenzied mood the deep impassion'd verse,
Ill-fated Bard! from each frail hope remove,
And shun the certain Suicide of Love:
Lean not to me, *th' impassion'd verse is o'er,*
Which chain'd thy heart, and forced thee to adore:
For O! observe where haughty Duty stands,
    Her form in radiance drest, her eye severe,
Eternal Scorpions writhing in her hands,
    To urge th' offender's *unavailing* tear!
Dread Goddess, I obey!—
Ah! smoothe thy awful terror-striking brow,
Hear and record MATILDA's sacred vow!
Ne'er will I quit th' undeviating *line,*
Whose SOURCE THOU art, and THOU the LAW DIVINE.
The Sun shall be subdued, his system fade,
Ere I forsake the path thy FIAT made;
Yet grant one soft regretful tear to flow,
Prompted by pity for a Lover's woe,

O grant *without* REVENGE, one bursting sigh,
Ere from his desolating grief I fly—
'Tis past,—Farewell!   ANOTHER claims my heart :
Then wing thy sinking steps, for here we part,
We PART! and listen, for the word is MINE,
ANNA MATILDA NEVER CAN BE THINE!"

THE INTERVIEW.

HANNAH COWLEY ("ANNA MATILDA")

(1743–1809)

Mrs. Cowley, in spite of her Della Cruscan hysterics, was no fool. She married a captain in the East India Company's service, and one night in February 1776, yawning by his side in a London theatre, was impelled to cry aloud what has so often been cried before: "Why, *I* could write as well as that!" Her husband grunted, but Hannah sat down to her escritoire on returning home and in a fortnight had finished her first play, *The Runaway*, which Garrick immediately accepted and produced at Drury Lane. From this time Mrs. Cowley was a leading playwright. Some of her comedies are by no means despicable, and are much above the depressing theatre of her day. Ellen Terry, Kemble, and Irving played in revivals of her principal success, *The Belle's Stratagem*.

Her platonic amour with Merry began in 1787 with the publication of his first poem, *Adieu and Recall to Love*, in the *World*. She answered it, signing herself "Anna Matilda." He replied. A preposterous exchange took place thenceforth, until in 1789 Della Crusca and Anna Matilda met face to face, for the first time. She was forty-six, he thirty-four. One more poem, *diminuendo*, emerged on either side after this meeting, and the affair ended.

Henry Morley has a judicious comment on Anna Matilda's Muse. "The quantity of agony taken at a meal by this favourite child of Fancy," he says, referring to the last line of the first extract following, "is grievous. Perhaps it might dispose some sympathetic reader to aim a third drop at the sod—if still to be found—on which Anna Matilda took such pains to hit with a tear of her own the same bit of dust that was wetted by a tear of Della Crusca's, as herein set forth."

She is said to have had a bright, piquant face.

Off Duty

I HATE the tardy elegiac lay—
Choose me a measure jocund as the day! . . .
And be thy lines irregular and free,
Poetic chains should fall before such bards as thee
Scorn the full laws that pinch thee round,
Raising above thy verse a mound,
O'er which thy Muse, so lofty! dares not bound.
Bid her in verse meand'ring sport;
Her footsteps quick, or long, or short,
Just as her various impulse wills—
Scorning the frigid square, which her fine fervour
            chills. . . .

And in thy verse meand'ring wild,
Thou, who art Fancy's favourite child,
May'st sweetly paint the long past hour,
When, the slave of Cupid's power,
Thou couldst the tear of rapture weep,
And feed on agony, and banish sleep.

                                    To DELLA CRUSCA.

The Well-Aimed Tear

O SYMPATHY, of birth divine,
Descend, and round my heart-strings twine!
Touch the fine nerve, whene'er I breathe
Where Della Crusca dropt his wreath!
Lead me the sacred way of Rome,
Lead me to kneel at Virgil's tomb,
Where he th' enduring marble round
With fresh-wove laurels, graceful bound.
Then guide where still with sweeter note
Than flowed from Petrarch's tuneful throat,

On Laura's grave he poured the lay
Amidst the sighs of sinking day:
Then point where on the sod his tear
Fell from its crystal source so clear,
That there my mingling tear may sink,
And the same dust its moisture drink.

TO DELLA CRUSCA.

DELLA CRUSCANS (*fl.* 1785–92)

OF these brief extracts from the verse of the Della Cruscan School the most vital is perhaps the last, which admirably echoes the disgust which the baseness of foreigners must ever awake in a British bosom, and is incidentally a striking plea for Thomas Cook (and Son), who arose some years later.

Of their number WILLIAM PARSONS (*fl.* 1785–1807) is chiefly notable because he complained bitterly to Gifford at being left out of the *Baviad* (1794), a slashing attack on the Della Cruscan coterie. Gifford, perceiving him to be a sincere coxcomb, admitted him. "This reference," said Gifford subsequently, "had a most fatal effect upon his poor head, and from an honest painstaking gentleman converted him in imagination into a Minotaur."

Moods

I

PLUCK from their dark and rocky bed
  The yelling demons of the deep,
Who soaring o'er the comet's head
  The bosom of the welkin sweep.

A DELLA CRUSCAN.

II

O pensive Passenger! do not deny
  To pause awhile, and weep upon the Tomb;
For here the cold remains of Campbell lie—
  This narrow spot the vernal Maiden's doom.

"AMICUS."

124

III

O blest with Taste, with Genius blest,
  Sole mistress of thy Bertie's breast,
Who to his love-enraptur'd arms art given,
The rich reward his virtues claim from Heaven!

WILLIAM PARSONS.

Notice to Tourists

But most avoid Italia's coast,
Where ev'ry sentiment is lost,
Where Treach'ry reigns, and base Disguise,
And Murder—looking to the skies,
While sordid Selfishness appears
In low redundancy of fears.
O! what can Music's voice bestow,
Or sculptur'd grace, or Titian glow,
To recompense the feeling mind
For British virtues left behind?

"LEONARDO."

MARY ROBINSON ("PERDITA") (1758–1800)

MARY ROBINSON, actress, poet, and *dame galante*, called by her admirers the English Sappho, derived much of her poetical success from her generous exploitation of personal amours in print, in the best modern manner. The most considerable of these was her affair in 1778 with the Prince of Wales, delicious in its preliminaries. The Prince, having surveyed the beautiful young leading lady once or twice from his box at Drury Lane and appraised her charms with all the cool and seasoned judgment of his sixteen years, stooped to conquer. A letter, signed "Florizel," was delivered to Mrs. Robinson by the hand of Lord Malden. She answered it in the name of Perdita, and very soon afterwards the lover and the lady met at Kew, chaperoned by the Duke of York, then Bishop of Osnaburgh. After one or two other rendezvous Perdita was officially appointed the Prince's *maîtresse en titre* with a bond for twenty thousand pounds, payable at George's coming of age, sealed with the Royal Arms of England, like a Bond Street confectioner's warrant.

Love waned in that fribble soul fairly soon and Perdita was discarded: the bond, naturally, was never honoured. Five years later Perdita was allowed five hundred a year by Charles James Fox, who became her lover, according to Horace Walpole, on her return to Brighton from a stay in Paris, where Marie-Antoinette had given the *belle Angloise* a purse netted by her own hands. She died, crippled and destitute, in a cottage in Surrey.

She was extremely lovely, vain, and fond of exhibition. Reynolds and Cosway each painted her twice, Gainsborough once; one of these portraits hangs in the Garrick Club. At the age of thirteen she was offered marriage by a breezy naval captain, but refused him for an articled clerk, Mr. Robinson, reputed to own property; the rigours of matrimony (and imprisonment for debt) she alleviated in the society of Lord Lyttelton and his dashing friends. She wrote a fair amount of verse, not all entirely despicable, one romance, and (according to Hazlitt) a pamphlet called *Thoughts on the Condition of Women*. A *Letter to the Women of England on the Injustice of Mental Subordination* has also been attributed to her.

The Temple of Chastity

HIGH on a rock, coeval with the skies,
   A temple stands, reared by immortal powers
   To Chastity divine!   Ambrosial flowers,
Twining round icicles, in columns rise,
Mingling with pendent gems of orient dyes!
   Piercing the air, a golden crescent towers,
   Veiled by transparent clouds; while smiling hours
Shake from their varying wings celestial joys!
The steps of spotless marble, scattered o'er
   With deathless roses armed with many a thorn,
Lead to the altar.   On the frozen floor,
   Studded with tear-drops, petrified with scorn,
Pale vestals kneel the goddess to adore,
   While Love, his arrows broke, retires forlorn.

            SAPPHO AND PHAON, SONNET II.

The Vest of Myrtle

BRING, bring to deck my brow, ye sylvan girls,
   A roseate wreath; nor for my waving hair
   The costly band of studded gems prepare,
Of sparkling chrysolite or orient pearls:
Love o'er my head his canopy unfurls,
   His purple pinions fan the whispering air;
   Mocking the golden sandal, rich and rare,
Beneath my feet the fragrant woodbine curls.

Bring the thin robe to fold about my breast,
   White as the downy swan; while round my waist
Let leaves of glossy myrtle bind the vest,
   Not idly gay, but elegantly chaste!
Love scorns the nymph in wanton trappings drest;
   And charms the most concealed are doubly graced.

                  Ibid., Sonnet XIII.

JOSEPH COTTLE (1770–1853)

BEFORE the age of twenty-one JOSEPH COTTLE had, it appears, read more than a thousand volumes of "the best English Literature." He nevertheless became a bookseller at Bristol in 1791, and has a certain title to celebrity as the early publisher and friend of Coleridge, Southey, and Wordsworth. In 1799 he retired from the book trade, in 1801 wrote (as was then the custom) an Epic Poem on Alfred, and in 1837 produced the more noteworthy *Early Recollections, chiefly relating to Samuel Taylor Coleridge.* In these memoirs Mr. Cottle is perceived to be a forerunner of what is known in our own time as the Cads' Concert. He had been impelled ("by vanity and self-righteousness," says his biographer) not only to set down his financial services to Southey and Coleridge but to expatiate in detail on Coleridge's addiction to drugging himself.

Cottle's other works, according to De Quincey, are two epic poems and a new kind of blacking.

Virtue Protests

FROM thy compeers in genius wisely learn:
From which of Southey's lines must virtue turn?
(Who, bold with Hell's vicegerents war to wage,
Brands the "Satanic school" to every age;
His visitings, Herculean, chief descending
Upon the "Head and front of the offending.")
Which verse shall Wordsworth ever blush to own?
Or Coleridge? spirit still of height unknown.
What tongue of Scotland's regal bard shall say,
Poison with pleasure mingles in his lay?
When shall Montgomery baneful lines bewail?
Or Crabbe? who haunts us like a nursery tale;
Bowles? Rogers? Barton? rich in Nature's store;
Or Campbell? would that I could add, or Moore!

EPISTLE TO LORD BYRON.

Ratiocinative

STILL I toil.
How long and steep and cheerless the ascent!
It needs the evidence of close deduction
To know that I shall ever reach the height!

THE MALVERN HILLS.

The Affectionate Heart

EVEN Genius may weary the sight
By too fierce and too constant a blaze;
But Affection, mild planet of night,
Grows lovelier the longer we gaze. . . .

When Time, at the end of his race,
Shall expire with expiring mankind,
It shall stand on its permanent base,
It shall last till the wreck of the mind.

ROBERT SOUTHEY (1774–1843)

THOUGH *Thalaba* and *The Curse of Kehama* are probably not read now as formerly, SOUTHEY was not only a generous and industrious man but in some ways a considerable poet. Westminster led him, Balliol fed him, and Coleridge converted him to Unitarian Pantisocracy; in addition to which he enjoyed the privilege of practically supporting Coleridge's family, with his own, for a long time by the work of his unaided pen. He was Poet Laureate from 1813; he refused the editorship of *The Times* with a salary of two thousand pounds a year —probably because he felt he was not good enough, in the higher sense; he wrote a History of the Peninsular War without the principal military documents, which the Duke refused to lend him, and held they did not matter; he declined Peel's offer of a baronetcy; and having married a second time in 1839, returned from his wedding tour, says the *Dictionary of National Biography* ungallantly, "in a condition of utter mental exhaustion." His faults, if they can be so called, were predicting national ruin on small provocation and believing all who differed from him politically to be enemies of God and society.

George III Enters Paradise

LIFT up your heads, ye Gates; and ye everlasting Portals,
Be ye lift up! For lo! a glorified Monarch approacheth,
One who in righteousness reign'd, and religiously govern'd
    his people.
Who are these that await him within? . . .

[*A select list follows: William III, Charles I, Elizabeth, Edward VI, the Black Prince, Edward III, Richard I, Alfred the Great.*]

I could perceive the joy which fill'd their beatified spirits
While of the Georgian Age they thought, and the glory of
    England.

A VISION OF JUDGMENT, VIII.

131

JAMES HENRY LEIGH HUNT (1784–1859)

ONE of the principal incidents in the full career of LEIGH HUNT, the cheerful, the resolute, the imprudent, the charming essayist, may be worth recollection here. In 1812 the *Morning Post*, a day or so after the toast of the Prince Regent had been ostentatiously passed over at a political dinner in London, printed a poetic exercise bordering on the fulsome in which George was hailed Protector of the Arts, Mæcenas of the Age, Glory of his People, and Adonis of Loveliness, attended by Pleasure, Honour, Virtue, and Truth. The comment of the *Examiner*, edited by Leigh Hunt and his brother John, was terse. It began: "This Adonis of Loveliness is a corpulent man of fifty. This delightful, blissful, wise, honourable, virtuous, true and immortal Prince is a violator of his word, a libertine over head and ears in disgrace, a despiser of domestic ties, the companion of gamblers and demireps. . . ." The result of printing what everybody knew was a sentence of two years' imprisonment and a fine of five hundred pounds. Leigh Hunt's stay in the Surrey Gaol was fairly pleasant, like Galileo's in the Inquisition: his room was brightly papered with a design of roses, his ceiling was sky-blue, he was surrounded by flowers, books, magazines, newspapers, his family, and visiting friends: he even had a pianoforte.

It was in prison that *The Story of Rimini* was written. The judgment of an eminent German critic that the fifteenth line of our first extract should read:

"'Excuse my glove,' said he:—it made her start,—"
is now accepted only in Upper Norwood. Perhaps Theodore Hook summed up the whole poem not inaccurately when he fathered on Byron the observation:

> "O crimini!
> What a nimini-pimini
> Story of Rimini!"

Lovers' Exchange

READY she sat with one hand to turn o'er
The leaf, to which her thoughts ran on before,
The other on the table, half enwreath'd
In the thick tresses over which she breath'd.
So sat she fix'd, and so observ'd was she
Of one, who at the door stood tenderly,—
Paolo,—who from a window seeing her
Go straight across the lawn, and guessing where,
Had thought she was in tears, and found, that
    day,
His usual efforts vain to keep away.
Twice had he seen her since the Prince was gone,
On some small matter needing unison;
Twice linger'd, and convers'd, and grown long
    friends;
But not till now where no one else attends.—
"May I come in?" said he:—it made her start,—
That smiling voice;—she colour'd, press'd her
    heart
A moment, as for breath, and then with free
And usual tone said,—"O yes, certainly."

                THE STORY OF RIMINI.

Domestic Chat

Ginevra (cheerfully). The world seems glad after its
    hearty drink
  Of rain. I feared, when you came back this morning,
The shower had stopped you, or that you were ill.
Ago. You feared!—you hoped. What fear you that I
    fear,
  Or hope for that I hope for? A truce, madam,
To these exordiums and pretended interests,

Whose only shallow intent is to delay,
Or to divert, the sole dire subject,—me.
Soh! you would see the spectacle! you, who start
At openings of doors and falls of pins.
Trumpets and drums quiet a lady's nerves,
And a good hacking blow at a tournament
Equals burnt feathers or hartshorn for a stimulus
To pretty household tremblers.

Gin.   I expressed
No wish to see the tournament, nor indeed
Anything, of my own accord, or contrary
To your good judgment.

Ago.   Oh, of course not.   Wishes
Are never expressed for, or by, contraries;
Nor the good judgment of an anxious husband
Held forth as a pleasant thing to differ with.

Gin. It is as easy as sitting in a chair
To say I will not go; and I will not.
Be pleased to think that settled.

                              A LEGEND OF FLORENCE.

"What with This and That——"

HE went to Arthur's Court, and play'd his part
So rarely, and display'd so frank a heart,
That what with all his charms of look and limb,
The Queen Geneura fell in love with him.

                              THE STORY OF RIMINI.

Aphrodite Adiposa

"LADY BLESSINGTON!" cried the glad usher aloud,
As she swam through the doorway, like moon from a
    cloud.
I know not which most her face beam'd with,—fine
    creature!
Enjoyment, or judgment, or wit, or good-nature.
Perhaps you have known what it is to feel longings
To pat buxom shoulders at routs and such throngings;—
Well,—think what it was, at a vision like that!
A Grace after dinner!—a Venus grown fat.

BLUE STOCKING REVELS.

HENRY KIRKE WHITE (1785–1806)

KIRKE WHITE, the son of a Nottingham butcher, had revealed a remarkable gift for languages, the classical especially, before his *Clifton Grove*, published in 1803 with a dedication to the Duchess of Devonshire, was seized on by Southey and praised with more enthusiasm than care. In 1805 White's undoubted piety, of a constricted type peculiar to his environment and period, procured him a sizarship at Cambridge by the interest of the benevolent Simeon, and it was in his rooms at St. John's, on the threshold of a brilliant career, that he died in the next year.

From the lines following it would appear no great pleasure for a poet to take an evening walk. "Don't talk about trouble," as the Duchess said to Alice. Blasts blow round him, horror stalks athwart the gloom, hags glare, a dying wanderer screams faintly in the distance, anguish gnaws him, tears roll down his emaciated cheek. How different, as the old lady might have said, is the home-life of the stockbroker.

Observe in the second extract an unwilling tribute to the regular habits of the industrial classes. Observe, in the third, Britannia's plight, to which the old sea-chantey might so well adapt itself:

"Hey! ho! Throw the girl back!"

Southey admired such verse, Byron was sympathetic, and Kirke White's posthumous poems and hymns went into ten editions.

The Evening Stroll

QUICK o'er the wintry waste dart fiery shafts—
  Bleak blows the blast—now howls—then faintly dies—
And oft upon its awful wing it wafts
  The dying wanderer's distant, feeble cries.

136

Now, when athwart the gloom gaunt horror stalks,
  And midnight hags their damnèd vigils hold,
The pensive Poet 'mid the wild waste walks,
  And ponders o'er the ills life's paths unfold.
Mindless of dangers hovering round, he goes,
  Insensible to every outward ill;
Yet oft his bosom heaves with rending throes,
  And oft big tears adown his wan cheeks trill.
Ah! 'tis the anguish of a mental sore,
Which gnaws his heart and bids him hope no more.

THE POET.

The Evening Sin

Now, when the rustic wears the social smile,
Released from day and its attendant toil,
And draws his household round their evening fire,
  And tells the oft-told tales that never tire:
Or where the town's blue turrets dimly rise,
And manufacture taints the ambient skies,
The pale mechanic leaves the labouring loom,
The air-pent hold, the pestilential room,
And rushes out, impatient to begin
The stated course of customary sin:
Now, now, my solitary way I bend
Where solemn groves in awful state impend,
And cliffs, that boldly rise above the plain,
Bespeak, blest Clifton, thy sublime domain.

CLIFTON GROVE.

Britannia Rejecta

WHERE now is Britain?—where her laurelled names,
Her palaces and halls?   Dashed in the dust.
Some second Vandal hath reduced her pride,
And with one big recoil hath thrown her back

To primitive barbarity.—Again,
Through her depopulated vales, the scream
Of bloody superstition hollow rings,
And the scared native to the tempest howls
The yell of deprecation.

TIME.

GEORGE GORDON, LORD BYRON (1788–1824)

Not immediately did Byron shock his eager countrymen with splendid cynicism, Satanism, and revolt. The early verses in rocking-horse metre which follow (and which he carefully preserved) are as blameless and affecting as Eliza Cook; the vision of the sailor bending over the Atlantic wave and dropping a tear of sensibility is equalled only by that of the soldier conscientiously weeping over his foeman's wounds, one tear for each gash. The Della Cruscan influence is perceptible.

Had Byron not died in glory at Missolonghi we might possibly have had much more of this kind of verse from him in his decline. Mr. Max Beerbohm has admirably pictured him as a florid old gentleman with iron-grey whiskers writing very long and able letters to *The Times* on the Corn Laws, and much exacerbated by Queen Victoria's refusal to sanction his appointment to a post in Lord John Russell's government.

The Tear

When Friendship or Love our sympathies move,
　　When Truth in a glance should appear,
The lips may beguile with a dimple or smile,
　　But the test of affection's a Tear. . . .

The man doom'd to sail with the blast of the gale,
　　Through billows Atlantic to steer,
As he bends o'er the wave which may soon be his grave,
　　The green sparkles bright with a Tear.

The soldier braves death for a fanciful wreath
　　In Glory's romantic career;
But he raises the foe when in battle laid low,
　　And bathes every wound with a Tear.

139

If with high-bounding pride he return to his bride,
  Renouncing the gore-crimson'd spear,
All his toils are repaid when, embracing the maid,
  From her eyelid he kisses the Tear. . . .

Ye friends of my heart, ere from you I depart,
  This hope to my breast is most near:
If again we shall meet in this rural retreat,
  May we meet, as we part, with a Tear.

When my soul wings her flight to the regions of night,
  And my corse shall recline on its bier,
As ye pass by the tomb where my ashes consume,
  Oh! moisten their dust with a Tear.

May no marble bestow the splendour of woe,
  Which the children of vanity rear;
No fiction of fame shall blazon my name;
  All I ask—all I wish—is a Tear.

HOURS OF IDLENESS.

The Prisoner Scolds

For he would never thus have flown,
And left me twice so doubly lone,—
Lone—as the corse within its shroud,
Lone—as a solitary cloud,
  A single cloud on a sunny day,
While all the rest of heaven is clear,
A frown upon the atmosphere,
That hath no business to appear
  When skies are blue, and earth is gay.

THE PRISONER OF CHILLON.

Cæsar Sings

I

To horse! to horse! my coal-black steed
   Paws the ground and snuffs the air!
There's not a foal of Arab's breed
   More knows what he must bear;
On the hill he will not tire,
Swifter as it waxes higher;
In the marsh he will not slacken,
On the plain be overtaken;
In the wave he will not sink,
Nor pause at the brook's side to drink;
In the race he will not pant,
In the combat he'll not faint;
On the stones he will not stumble,
Time nor toil will make him humble;
In the stall he will not stiffen,
But be wingèd as a griffin,
Only flying with his feet:
And will not such a voyage be sweet?
Merrily, merrily, never unsound,
Shall our bonny black horses skim over the ground!
From the Alps to the Caucasus, ride we or fly!
For we'll leave them behind in the glance of an eye.

THE DEFORMED TRANSFORMED, ACT I, Sc. II.

II

WHEN the lion was young,
   In the pride of his might,
Then 'twas sport for the strong
   To embrace him in fight;
To go forth, with a pine
   For a spear, 'gainst the mammoth,

Or strike through the ravine
  At the foaming Behemoth;
While man was in stature
  As towers in our time,
The first-born of Nature,
  And like her, sublime!

IBID., ACT III Sc. I.

WILLIAM WORDSWORTH (1770–1850)

THE reason why a poet of the stature of WILLIAM WORDSWORTH produced verse of the kind which follows has been amply debated by his admirers and others; some have accounted for it by Naturalism, others by Neo-Pantheism, others by the French Revolution, others by the depressing scenery of the Lake District, and others, again, by his more recently-revealed elective and Platonic affinity with a young French maiden, Annette Vallon; an idyll distinguished by true Wordsworthian rectitude, elevation, and propriety, though certain persons have dared to attach to it hints of a less serious sentiment. Such hints we will (in Mrs. Boffin's presence) merely dismiss with the contempt they merit. Annette's child was a girl.

Wordsworth, in addition to being one of the greatest English poets, was also one of our most efficient Distributors of Stamps for Cumberland and Westmorland, as was officially acknowledged at the time. In appearance he was over average height, large-boned, somewhat clumsy, with a heavy mouth, a prominent nose, and glowing eyes: hence his surname Hippokephalos, or Horse-Face.

The verses following should be sipped, not gulped. The compilers take some modest pride in pointing out, probably for the first time in the history of English poetry, that Wordsworth's lines on the leech-gatherer anticipated by some years the strikingly similar lines of another poet of distinction:

> "I shook him well from side to side
> Until his face was blue.
> 'Come, tell me how you live,' I cried,
> 'And what it is you do.'
> He said, 'I hunt for haddocks' eyes
> Among the heather bright'" (*etc.*).

The same author supplies the necessary gloss for Stanza 7 of *The Old Huntsman*:—"'Everything's got a moral,' said the Duchess." And in connection with the worm's indifference to feather-beds, justly noted by Wordsworth, a keen observer of wild life, may direct the reader's attention to Cowley's remarks on the more sybaritic frog in *The Plagues of Egypt*:

> "Insatiate yet they mount up higher,
> Where never sun-born Frog durst to aspire,
> And in the silken beds their slimy members place,
> A luxury unknown before to all the wat'ry race."

Odd Case of Mr. Gill

Oh! what's the matter? what's the matter?
What is't that ails young Harry Gill?
That evermore his teeth they chatter,
Chatter, chatter, chatter still!
Of waistcoats Harry has no lack,
Good duffle grey, and flannel fine;
He has a blanket on his back,
And coats enough to smother nine.

In March, December, and in July,
'Tis all the same with Harry Gill;
The neighbours tell, and tell you truly,
His teeth they chatter, chatter still.
At night, at morning, and at noon,
'Tis all the same with Harry Gill;
Beneath the sun, beneath the moon,
His teeth they chatter, chatter still.

GOODY BLAKE AND HARRY GILL

(Oxford Street ?)

An Orpheus! an Orpheus! yes, Faith may grow bold,
And take to himself all the wonders of old;—
Near the stately Pantheon you'll meet with the same
In the street that from Oxford hath borrow'd its name.

THE POWER OF MUSIC.

The Aged, Aged Man

My question eagerly did I renew,
"How is it that you live, and what is it you do?"
He with a smile did then his words repeat;
And said, that, gathering leeches, far and wide
He travelled; stirring thus about his feet
The waters of the pools where they abide.
"Once I could meet with them on every side;
But they have dwindled long by slow decay;
Yet still I persevere, and find them where I may."

RESOLUTION AND INDEPENDENCE.

Asked and Answered

——HAST thou then survived—
Mild offspring of infirm humanity,
Meek infant! among all forlornest things
The most forlorn—one life of that bright star,
The second glory of the Heavens?—Thou hast.

ADDRESS TO MY INFANT DAUGHTER.

The Old Huntsman

IN the sweet shire of Cardigan
Not far from pleasant Ivor-hall,
An old Man dwells, a little man,—
'Tis said he once was tall.
Of years he has upon his back,
No doubt a burden weighty;
He says he is three score and ten,
But others say he's eighty.

A long blue livery-coat has he,
That's fair behind and fair before;
Yet, meet him when you will, you see
At once that he is poor.

Full five-and-thirty years he lived
A running huntsman merry;
And though he has but one eye left,
His cheek is like a cherry. . . .

And he is lean and he is sick,
His little body's half awry,
His ankles they are swollen and thick;
His legs are thin and dry.
When he was young he little knew
Of husbandry or tillage,
And now he's forced to work, though weak,
—The weakest of the village.

One prop he has, and only one,
His wife, an aged woman,
Lives with him, near the waterfall,
Upon the village Common. . . .

Oft, working by her Husband's side,
Ruth does what Simon cannot do;
For she, with scanty cause for pride,
Is stouter of the two.
And though you with your utmost skill
From labour could not wean them,
'Tis little, very little—all
That they can do between them.

Few months of life has he in store
As he to you will tell,
For still, the more he works, the more
Do his weak ankles swell.
My gentle Reader, I perceive
How patiently you've waited,
And now I fear that you'll expect
Some tale will be related.

O Reader! had you in your mind
Such stores as silent thought could bring,
O gentle Reader! you would find
A tale in every thing.
What more I have to say is short,
And you must kindly take it:
It is no tale; but, should you think,
Perhaps a tale you'll make it.

One summer-day I chanced to see
This old man doing all he could
To unearth the root of an old tree,
A stump of rotten wood.
The mattock tottered in his hand;
So vain was his endeavour,
That at the root of the old tree
He might have worked for ever.

"You're overtasked, good Simon Lee,
Give me your tool," to him I said;
And at the word right gladly he
Received my proffered aid.
I struck, and with a single blow
The tangled root I severed,
At which the poor old Man so long
And vainly had endeavoured.

SIMON LEE
(ORIGINAL VERSION).

The Poet Reveals All

HIGH on a mountain's highest ridge,
Where oft the stormy winter gale
Cuts like a scythe, while through the clouds
It sweeps from vale to vale;
Not five yards from the mountain path,
This Thorn you on your left espy;

And to the left, three yards beyond,
You see a little muddy pond,
Though but of compass small, and bare
To thirsty suns and parching air.
I've measured it from side to side;
'Tis three feet long, and two feet wide. . . .

Nay, rack your brain—'tis all in vain,
I'll tell you every thing I know;
But to the Thorn, and to the pond
Which is a little step beyond,
I wish that you would go:
Perhaps, when you are at the place,
You something of her tale may trace.

I'll give you the best help I can:
Before you up the mountain go,
Up to the dreary mountain-top,
I'll tell you all I know.
'Tis now some two-and-twenty years
Since she (her name is Martha Ray)
Gave, with a maiden's true good will,
Her company to Stephen Hill;
And she was blithe and gay,
And she was happy, happy still
Whene'er she thought of Stephen Hill.

And they had fixed the wedding day,
The morning that must wed them both;
But Stephen to another Maid
Had sworn another oath;
And with this other Maid, to church
Unthinking Stephen went—
Poor Martha! on that woeful day
A cruel, cruel fire, they say,

William Wordsworth, in the Lake District, at Cross-purposes

Into her bones was sent:
It dried her body like a cinder,
And almost turned her brain to tinder.

THE THORN (ORIGINAL VERSION).

Baffled

"Now, little Edward, say why so:
My little Edward, tell me why."—
"I cannot tell, I do not know."—
"Why, this is strange," said I.

ANECDOTE FOR FATHERS.

The Course Prescribed

[*The Vicar is telling of one who has been advised by a friend to take up botany as a cure for unrequited love. He pauses to moralise.*]

"THE attempt was made;—'tis needless to report
How hopelessly; but innocence is strong,
And an entire simplicity of mind
A thing most sacred in the eye of Heaven;
That opens, for such sufferers, relief
Within the soul, fountains of grace divine;
And doth commend their weakness and disease
To Nature's care, assisted in her office
By all the elements that round her wait
To generate, to preserve, and to restore;
And by her beautiful array of forms
Shedding sweet influence from above; or pure
Delight exhaling from the ground they tread."

"Impute it not to impatience, if," exclaimed
The Wanderer, "I infer that he was healed
By perseverance in the course prescribed."[1]

THE EXCURSION.

A Mother's Quest

AND thus continuing, she said,
"I had a son, who many a day
Sailed on the sea; but he is dead;
In Denmark he was cast away;
And I have travelled far as Hull to see
What clothes he might have left, or other property."

THE SAILOR'S MOTHER
(ORIGINAL VERSION).

Insensibility

THE beetle loves his unpretending track,
The snail the house he carries on his back;
The far-fetched worm with pleasure would disown
The bed we give him, though of softest down.

LIBERTY.

The Stuffed Owl

[*This is taken from the account given by Miss Jewsbury of the pleasure she derived, when long confined to her bed by sickness, from the inanimate object on which this Sonnet turns.—W. W.*]

WHILE Anna's peers and early playmates tread,
In freedom, mountain-turf and river's marge;
Or float with music in the festal barge;
Rein the proud steed, or through the dance are led;
Her doom it is to press a weary bed—

[1] He was; but he caught a fever and died, bequeathing his herbarium to his lost love.

Till oft her guardian Angel, to some charge
More urgent called, will stretch his wings at large,
And friends too rarely prop the languid head.
Yet, helped by Genius—untired Comforter,
The presence even of a stuffed Owl for her
Can cheat the time; sending her fancy out
To ivied castles and to moonlight skies,
Though he can neither stir a plume, nor shout;
Nor veil, with restless film, his staring eyes.

Decadence ; or, The Umbrella

THE pibroch's note, discountenanced or mute;
The Roman kilt, degraded to a toy
Of quaint apparel for a half-spoilt boy;
The target mouldering like ungathered fruit;
The smoking steam-boat eager in pursuit,
As eagerly pursued; the umbrella spread
To weather-fend the Celtic herdsman's head—
All speak of manners withering to the root,
And of old honours, too, and passions high:
Then may we ask, though pleased that thought should
    range
Among the conquests of civility,
Survives imagination—to the change
Superior?   Help to virtue does she give?
If not, O mortals, better cease to live!

YARROW REVISITED.

A Worm's Life Not Everything

SEE where his difficult way that Old Man wins,
Bent by a load of Mulberry leaves! most hard
Appears *his* lot, to the small Worm's compared,
For whom his toil with early day begins.
Acknowledging no task-master, at will
(As if her labour and her ease were twins)

She seems to work, at pleasure to lie still;—
And softly sleeps within the thread she spins.
So fare they—the Man serving as her Slave.
Ere long their fates do each to each conform:
Both pass into new being,—but the Worm,
Transfigured, sinks into a hopeless grave;
His volant spirit will, he trusts, ascend
To bliss unbounded, glory without end.

MEMORIALS OF A TOUR IN ITALY.

An Experiment that Failed

To a lodge that stood
Deep in a forest, with leave given, at the age
Of four-and-twenty summers he withdrew;
And thither took with him his motherless Babe,
And one domestic for their common needs,
An aged woman. It consoled him here
To attend upon the orphan, and perform
Obsequious service to the precious child,
Which, after a short time, by some mistake
Or indiscretion of the Father, died.

VAUDRACOUR AND JULIA.

JOHN KEATS (1795-1821)

To reproduce the early half-awakened pipings of JOHN KEATS
which follow may seem at a first glance unjust; but they are
included in his collected works (for like Byron and Burns
he thought such things worthy of being preserved) and are
therefore eligible.

The marvellous note of Keats's riper genius was inspired
largely by Miss Fanny Brawne of Hampstead, a young, fair
lady, slightly capricious in a nice way, who was much afflicted
by the poet's untimely death and afterwards married a
Mr. Lindo, who changed his name to Lindon and was one of
the secretaries of the Great Exhibition, 1851.

To Some Ladies

WHAT though while the wonders of nature exploring,
  I cannot your light, mazy footsteps attend;
Nor listen to accents, that almost adoring,
  Bless Cynthia's face, the enthusiast's friend:

Yet over the steep, whence the mountain stream rushes,
  With you, kindest friends, in idea I muse;
Mark the clear tumbling crystal, its passionate gushes,
  In spray that the wild flower kindly bedews. . . .

'Tis morn, and the flowers with dew are yet drooping,
  I see you are treading the verge of the sea:
And now! ah, I see it—you just now are stooping
  To pick up the keepsake intended for me.

If a cherub, on pinions of silver descending,
  Had brought me a gem from the fretwork of heaven;
And smiles, with his star-cheering voice sweetly blending,
  The blessing of Tighe had melodiously given;

It had not created a warmer emotion
    Than the present, fair nymph, I was blest with from
        you,
Than the shell, from the bright golden sands of the ocean,
    Which the emerald waves at your feet gladly threw.

For, indeed, 'tis a sweet and peculiar pleasure,
    (And blissful is he who such happiness finds,)
To possess but a span of the hour of leisure,
    In elegant, pure and aerial minds.

CORNELIUS WHUR (1782–1853)

THE REV. CORNELIUS WHUR was unrepresented in the majestic *corpus* of English Poetry until some few years ago Mr. E. V. Lucas retrieved from Limbo and reprinted *The Female Friend*, whose charms require no fingerpost. Little enough is known of the mild poet himself, save that according to *The Norfolk Garland* he "followed the business of a gardener, and in early life became a Wesleyan minister. . . . He was patronised by many clergymen, and Dr. Hall, rector of Gulbourne, Cambs., was a great friend to him." He is buried at Pulham Market, having "gone foreign" about 1845 and moved from Pulham in Norfolk to Bungay in Suffolk, where he died. On this account the *Gentleman's Magazine* obituary for May 1853 styles him "the Suffolk Poet," which is clearly monstrous. It was at Pulham St. Mary Magdalen, near Harleston in Norfolk, that Mr. Whur composed for publication in 1837, and again in 1845, a volume of poems—*Village Musings on Moral and Religious Subjects* and *Gratitude's Offering, being Original Productions on a Variety of Subjects*. Both volumes were published at Norwich by subscription. Mr. Whur's preface to *Gratitude's Offering* contains this passage:

> "The *title* which this volume bears was adopted by the author in consequence of the unanticipated *patronage* he has received—the success that attended his former work, *Village Musings, three* large editions having been called for in a very short time. . . . To ladies and gentlemen who adorn the first circles he considers himself under special obligations.
>
> "The life of the writer, he may observe, has been rather eventful, and he cannot but say that the encouragement he has received from the Rev. Dr. Hall forms one of the most gratifying circumstances of his history."

Dr. Hall's encouragement was not unmerited, for Mr. Whur was no Puseyite, and seems indeed amid his musings on moral and religious subjects to have been entirely oblivious of the upheavals of the Oxford Movement; to this no doubt he owed some of the approbation of the ladies and gentlemen of the first circles, including Mr. Joseph John Gurney, the Quaker philanthropist, who took two copies. In the considerable army of extinct spinsters and clergymen who have enriched English literature with volumes of poetry and "pamphlets about growing roses and resisting sin," the Rev. Cornelius Whur must henceforth occupy commanding rank, and his unknown polished female friend (*dulce politam*) will become as dear to lovers of urbane poetry as Lalage—with the added attraction that she was undoubtedly flesh and blood, whereas all Horace's female friends, polished and other, were, happily, as a virtuous English Don proved in print a few years ago, wholly imaginary.

The Female Friend

In this imperfect, gloomy scene
  Of complicated ill,
How rarely is a day serene,
  The throbbing bosom still!
Will not a beauteous landscape bright,
  Or music's soothing sound,
Console the heart, afford delight,
  And throw sweet peace around?
They may, but never comfort lend
Like an accomplish'd female friend!

With such a friend, the social hour
  In sweetest pleasure glides;
There is in female charms a power
  Which lastingly abides—
The fragrance of the blushing rose,
  Its tints and splendid hue,
Will with the season decompose,
  And pass as flitting dew;
On firmer ties his joys depend
Who has a polish'd female friend!

The pleasures which from thence arise
  Surpass the blooming flower,
For though it opens to the skies,
  It closes in an hour!
Its sweetness is of transient date,
  Its varied beauties cease—
They can no lasting joys create,
  Impart no lasting peace;
While both arise, and duly blend
In an accomplish'd female friend!

As orbs revolve and years recede,
  As seasons onward roll,
The fancy may on beauties feed,
  With discontented soul!
A thousand objects bright and fair
  May for a moment shine,
Yet many a sigh and many a tear
  But mark their swift decline;
While lasting joys the man attend
Who has a faithful female friend!

The First-Rate Wife

This brief effusion I indite,
  And my vast wishes send,
That thou mayst be directed right,
And have ere long within thy sight
  A most *enchanting* friend!

The *maiden* should have *lovely face*,
  And be of *genteel mien*;
If not, within thy dwelling place,
There may be vestige of disgrace,
  Not much admired—when seen.

N

Nor will thy dearest be complete
　　Without *domestic* care;
If otherwise, howe'er discreet,
Thine eyes will very often meet
　　What none desire to share!

And further still—thy future *dear*,
　　Should have some *mental* ray;
If not, thou mayest drop a tear,
Because no *real sense* is there
　　To charm life's dreary day!

The Unfortunate Gentleman

[*Some time since the writer was introduced to a gentleman, who
politely requested his acceptance of a handsome walking-stick,
giving him at the same time its interesting history, which is as
follows : It had been the property, and daily companion of a
gentleman (a member of the Church of England), who although a
layman, most laudably employed several evenings in each week
preaching to, and instructing the peasantry in different cottages
in his neighbourhood. This gentleman, upon a certain occasion,
gathered what he supposed to be mushrooms, in eating which,
himself, a sister, and a little boy were poisoned.*—AUTHOR'S NOTE.]

HE, whose warm hand had often pressed
　　Thy smoothly rounded head,
Is where the "weary are at rest,"
　　There hath thine owner fled. . . .

And often as he leaned on thee
　　In copse, or flowery glen;
O! did he not in vision see
　　The wretchedness of men?

At other times, when lifting thee
　　In gay and curving swing,
'Twas his a brighter scene to see
　　And of that scene to sing.

Good as thou art, he clearly knew,
  Although thou wast his stay,
Thy virtues would recede from view,
  Thyself fall in decay. . . .

But in a dark and trying hour
  (Man hath his days of woe!),
He found in vegetable power
  A dreadful, deadly foe!

His heart corroded—sank to rest,
  No more to ope life's way;
His hand no longer on thee pressed,
  Thyself no more his stay!

He resteth where the nettles spring,
  Not having aid from thee;
On that account I of thee sing,
  Who now belongst to me!

From "*The Rose-Covered Grave*"

[*The author, in passing through a beautiful churchyard in the
county of Norfolk, was particularly struck with the appearance
of a recently covered grave, which was surrounded by a profusion
of roses. Afterwards, while proceeding on his journey he casually
overtook the gentleman whose lady had been interred in the grave
which had engaged his attention, and of whose sudden departure he
gave the following relation : He had an only daughter, who at the
period referred to was seriously indisposed, and who had been
deploring that circumstance in consequence of the inconvenience
it occasioned in the family. The lady, who at that time was in
perfect health, endeavoured to console the mind of her afflicted
daughter by exclaiming, "Thank God, I am quite well, and will
alleviate your sufferings !" But within twenty minutes the
affectionate mother, who had thus spoken, was a corpse, and in*

the above-named grave her remains were reposing.—AUTHOR'S
NOTE.]

THE morning arose, and its beauties were beaming,
   As they danced in her vision like snow-crested wave;
But alas! as such splendours were brilliantly gleaming.
   She retired to repose in the rose-covered grave!

That hour was a season of gloomy decision,
   For no merciful hand was uplifted to save;
Nor aught to illuminate the dark-clouded vision,
   As she stood on the brink of her rose-covered grave!

She'd heard too, to add to the keen separation,
   A long nurtured daughter despondently rave;
Nor could she but sigh for a *dearer* relation,
   Who would weep as she went to her rose-covered grave!

Yet she fell 'mid emotions of exquisite sorrow,
   So awfully did the grim monster behave;
And the sad apparatus was used on the morrow,
   To prepare for her rest in the rose-covered grave!

And there, as the breezes are wantonly playing,
   The beautiful buds will develop and wave;
And zephyrs will chance as their fragrance is straying
   To sweeten the scene of the rose-covered grave!

Catastrophe

[*The lines below were suggested by seeing an artist who was
born without arms, who supports himself and his parents also by
his profession.*—AUTHOR'S NOTE.]

"ALAS! alas!" the father said,
   "O what a dispensation!
How can we be by mercy led,
   In such a situation?
Be not surprised at my alarms,
The dearest boy is without arms! . . .

"I have no hope, no confidence,
  The scene around is dreary;
How can I meet such vast expense?
  I am by trying weary.
You must, my dearest, plainly see
This armless boy will ruin me."

THE ARMLESS ARTIST.

The Poet Questions the Ant

WHY did you, feeble as you were, attempt
A task so perfectly herculean?
Could it be to rear your tender offspring?
Did your concern touching their welfare
So impel? Was aught like conference held
Ere you began to calculate success? . . .
               Man, physically
Your superior, could not with equal tools
The work have done. He, comparatively,
Might as soon this ponderous earth divide.

VILLAGE MUSINGS.

And So Home

[*Two gentlemen, having met accidentally at an inn and having been detained by a shower of rain, part after a theological discussion.*]

JUST as he reach'd this stirring close,
The other gentleman arose;
And with emotion and surprise,
He rang the bell, then wip'd his eyes;
And ere he for his dwelling started,
His hand he held,—and thus they parted.

LIBERALITY OF SENTIMENT.

ROBERT POLLOK (1798–1827)

On the granite obelisk erected to the memory of Robert Pollok in a churchyard near Southampton are engraved the words: "His immortal Poem is his monument." The inscription refers to a poetical work of ten books in blank verse entitled *The Course of Time*, dealing with the destiny of man, published at Edinburgh in 1825; its immortality lasted until about 1867, when it reached its twenty-fifth edition.

Pollok, a Scottish farmer's son, entered the Presbyterian ministry from Glasgow University and died young. He distinguished himself while in the Academic Groves in logic and moral philosophy. As a poet he displays all the dour will-power popularly attributed to his race. In the first extract following the embarrassing situation of an anatomist caught unawares by the Last Day is graphically portrayed. In the third, one perceives an angel or two giving mankind what seems rather a brief supercilious glance, like Brummell at an evening party.

A Contretemps

And as the anatomist, with all his band
Of rude disciples, o'er the subject hung,
And impolitely hewed his way, through bones
And muscles of the sacred human form,
Exposing barbarously to wanton gaze
The mysteries of nature, joint embraced
His kindred joint, the wounded flesh grew up,
And suddenly the injured man awoke
Among their hands, and stood arrayed complete
In immortality—forgiving scarce
The insult offered to his clay in death.

THE COURSE OF TIME, BK. VII.

Proximities

THE Memphian mummy, that from age to age
Descending, bought and sold a thousand times,
In hall of curious antiquary stowed,
Wrapped in mysterious weeds, the wondrous theme
Of many an erring tale, shook off its rags;
And the brown son of Egypt stood beside
The European, his last purchaser.
In vale remote, the hermit rose, surprised
At crowds that rose around him, where he thought
His slumbers had been single; and the bard,
Who fondly covenanted with his friend,
To lay his bones beneath the sighing bough
Of some old lonely tree, rising, was pressed
By multitudes that claimed their proper dust
From the same spot; and he, that, richly hearsed,
With gloomy garniture of purchased wo,
Embalmed, in princely sepulchre was laid,
Apart from vulgar men, built nicely round
And round by the proud heir, who blushed to think
His father's lordly clay should ever mix
With peasant dust,—saw by his side awake
The clown that long had slumbered in his arms.

IBID.

The Once-Over

STILL, all was calm in heaven.   Nor yet appeared
The Judge, nor aught appeared, save here and there,
On wing of golden plumage borne at will
A curious angel, that from out the skies
Now glanced a look on man, and then retired.

IBID., BK. VIII.

RALPH WALDO EMERSON (1803–82)

THE bleak New England breeze which whistles through the justly-celebrated ethical works of RALPH WALDO EMERSON is noticeably absent from the lines which follow. The precise meaning of the first extract may be at first obscure, but in essence (and in style) it may be said to proclaim much the same stout message of cheer promulgated by later Nordic philosophers, among them Dr. Frank Crane, Mrs. Ella Wheeler Wilcox, and Mr. Al Jolson—this last with a black face.

Emerson was at one time a Unitarian pastor at Boston, Mass., that centre of culture and social exclusiveness where, as the classic couplet used to say:

> "The Lowells talk to the Cabots,
> And the Cabots talk only to God."

His collected poems were published in 1871. His earlier *Essays on Representative Men* are said by their admirers to equal anything of Carlyle.

Get-Together Song

EYES of gods! ye must have seen,
O'er your ramparts as you lean,
The general debility;
Of genius the sterility;
Mighty projects countermanded;
Rash ambition, broken-handed;
Puny man and scentless rose
Tormenting Pan to double the dose. . . .

We must have society,
We cannot spare variety.
Hear you, then, celestial fellows!
Fits not to be over-zealous;

Steads not to work on the clean jump,
Nor wine nor brains perpetual pump.
Men and gods are too extense;
Could you slacken and condense?
Your rank overgrowths reduce
Till your kinds abound in juice?

ALPHONSO OF CASTILE.

Efficiency

EARTH, crowded, cries: "Too many men!"
My counsel is, kill nine in ten,
And bestow the shares of all
On the remnant decimal.
Add their nine lives to this cat;
Stuff their nine brains in one hat;
Make his frame and forces square
With the labours he must dare;
Thatch his flesh, and even his years,
With the marble which he rears.
There, growing slowly old at ease,
No faster than his planted trees,
He may, by warrant of his age,
In schemes of broader scope engage.
So shall ye have a man of the sphere
Fit to grace the solar year.

IBID.

THOMAS HAYNES BAYLY (1797–1839)

Few British poets have had a more instant claim to the respect of the Island Race than Thomas Haynes Bayly, who was related on his mother's side to the Earl of Stamford and Warrington. Before the age of eight he had composed a drama. Relinquishing in due course his intention of entering the Established Church, he married (1826) Miss Hayes of Marble Hill, Co. Cork, and during a stay with his young bride at Lord Ashdown's villa on Southampton Water his ripening talent broke suddenly into song with the composition of *I'd Be a Butterfly*, in which a strong desire to flutter to and fro like that beautiful and colourful insect was very graphically expressed. The poem was written, says a biographer, "in romantic circumstances"—and one may be almost certain that the poet was gratified by the approval of Lord Ashdown himself, who added to singular munificence a true nobleman's patronage of letters, in so far as they are designed to improve public taste.

A three-volume novel, *The Aylmers*, followed; then numerous songs and ballads, which Mr. Bayly published in two volumes, entitling the one *Loves of the Butterflies*, but the other *Songs of the Old Château*. In 1831 the coal-mines in which the poet had financial interests became unhappily unproductive, but the publication of *The Bridesmaid* in that year drew "a flattering letter from Sir Robert Peel, and formed the subject of a remarkable picture by one of the leading artists of the day." Reproductions in colour of this picture, which finely depicted a bridesmaid in the situation ascribed to her in the poem, are no longer (we are informed by Messrs. Colnaghi) to be obtained.

Mr. Bayly composed in addition, some thirty-six dramatic pieces. His *Parliamentary Letters, and other Poems*, *Kindness in Women*, a collection of tales, and *Weeds of Witchery* were deservedly popular. Among his admirers was Mr. Richard Swiveller.

Oh, No! We Never Mention Her

Oh, no! we never mention her,
  Her name is never heard;
My lips are now forbid to speak
  That once familiar word;
From sport to sport they hurry me
  To banish my regret;
And when they win a smile from me [1]
  They think that I forget!

They bid me seek in change of scene
  The charms that others see,
But were I in a foreign land
  They'd find no change in me. [2]
'Tis true that I behold no more
  The valley where we met;
I do not see the hawthorn tree,
  But how can I forget?

They tell me she is happy now,
  The gayest of the gay;
They hint that she's forgotten me,
  But heed not what they say.
Like me, perhaps, she struggles with
  Each feeling of regret;
But if she loves as I have loved,
  She never can forget.

[1] *Var. lect.* supplied by Andrew Lang:
      "And when they only worry me."

[2] *Var. lect.:*
      "They'd get no change from me."

Something to Love

SOMETHING to love, some tree or flow'r,
Something to nurse in my lonely bow'r,
Some dog to follow, where'er I roam,
Some bird to warble my welcome home,
Some tame gazelle, or some gentle dove:
Something to love, oh, something to love!

Something to love, oh, let me see!
Something that's filled with a love for me;
Beloved by none, it is sad to live,
And 'tis sad to die and leave none to grieve;
And fond and true let the lov'd one prove.
Something to love, oh, something to love!

I'm Saddest When I Sing

You think I have a merry heart
    Because my songs are gay,
But oh! they all were taught to me
    By friends now far away:
The bird will breathe her silver note
    Though bondage binds her wing;—
But *is* her song a happy one?
    I'm saddest when I sing!

I heard them first in that sweet home
    I never more shall see,
And now each song of joy has got
    A mournful turn for me:
Alas! 'tis vain in winter time
    To mock the songs of spring,
Each note recalls some withered leaf—
    I'm saddest when I sing!

Of all the friends I used to love
   My harp remains alone;
Its faithful voice still seems to be
   An echo to my own:
My tears when I bend over it
   Will fall upon its string,
Yet those who hear me little think
   I'm saddest when I sing.

The Soldier's Tear

UPON a hill he turned,
   To take a last fond look
Of the valley and the village church,
   And the cottage by the brook.
He listened to the sounds
   So familiar to the ear,
And the soldier leant upon his sword
   And wiped away a tear. . . .

He turned and left the spot,
   Oh! do not deem him weak,
For dauntless was the soldier's heart,
   Tho' tears were on his cheek.
Go watch the foremost ranks,
   In danger's dark career.
Be sure the hand most daring there
   Has wiped away a tear.

I'd be a Butterfly

I'D be a Butterfly born in a bower,
   Where roses and lilies and violets meet;
Roving for ever from flower to flower,
   And kissing all buds that are pretty and sweet!

I'd never languish for wealth, or for power;
   I'd never sigh to see slaves at my feet:
I'd be a Butterfly born in a bower,
   Kissing all buds that are pretty and sweet. . . .

What, though you tell me each gay little rover
   Shrinks from the breath of the first autumn day!
Surely 'tis better, when summer is over,
   To die when all fair things are fading away.
Some in life's winter may toil to discover
   Means of procuring a weary delay—
I'd be a Butterfly; living, a rover,
   Dying when fair things are fading away.

ELIZABETH OAKES SMITH (1806–93)

Mrs. Smith, born at Portland, Mass., in 1806, moved after marriage to New York, where she contributed prose and verse to leading periodicals, including the *Southern Literary Messenger*, Poe's paper, in which *The Sinless Child* appeared in 1841. Her first collection of poems, a slim volume, was published two years later. "For the sake of poetry and the promotion of elevated views of life," wrote a Mr. Tuckerman, reviewing it, "we cannot mourn the destiny which made such a woman known to fame. . . . We hope, that not a few of her sex have hailed these manifestations in language of what is highest in their own souls."

With the assembly round little Eva of affectionate coleoptera and orthoptera may be compared the surly attitude of those in Grainger's *Sugar-Cane*:

> "Mosquitoes, sand-flies seek the shelter'd roof,
> And with fell rage the stranger-guest assail,
> Nor spare the sportive child; from their retreats
> Cockroaches crawl displeasingly abroad."

These would be capable of biting a sinless child. Not so the gentle and confiding gasteropods in Lytton's *Little Ella*:

> "The poor, pink snail
> Fear'd less your steps than those of the May showers;
> It is not strange these creatures loved you so,
> And told you all."

Insect Affection

And ere she left with tottling steps
The low-roofed cottage door,
The beetle and the cricket loved
The young child on the floor.

And every insect dwelt secure
  Where little Eva played;
And piped for her its blithest song
  When she in greenwood strayed.

With wing of gauze and mailèd coat
  They gathered round her feet,
Rejoiced, as are all gladsome things,
  A truthful soul to greet.
They taught her infant lips to sing
  With them a hymn of praise,
The song that in the woods is heard
  Through the long summer days.

THE SINLESS CHILD.

Walt Whitman, inciting the Bird of Freedom to Soar

ROBERT MONTGOMERY (1807–55)

ROBERT MONTGOMERY, born Gomery, had assumed the genteel prefix some time before his longish poem *The Omnipresence of the Deity*, dedicated to Bishop Howley, brought him fame in 1828. The poem was sufficiently divorced from all the lovely Graces, rich in elementary bathos and bombast, and steeped in the suburban religiosity of the period to find instant success with the British public and to run into eight editions in eight months. It was this, together with the frantic newspaper puffing which welcomed Mr. Montgomery's next two offerings—*A Universal Prayer : Death ; a Vision of Heaven ; and a Vision of Hell*, and *Satan, or Intellect without God*—which earned the complacent poet (whose editions were soon enriched with a frontispiece-portrait of himself with eyes lifted heavenwards, and resembling Byron as much as possible) the historic castigation by Macaulay in the *Edinburgh Review* of April 1830; an annihilating so Jove-like that the victim automatically commands the spectator's rueful sympathy. Mr. Montgomery, though for a moment he contemplated bringing a libel action, remained complacent, as well he might, for he held the evangelical market. *Omnipresence* reached twenty-eight editions by 1858.

His *Messiah*, in six books, dedicated to Queen Adelaide (1832), brought the respectable poet a medal, for the House of Saxe-Meiningen has ever encouraged the arts; and in 1833 Mr. Montgomery published *Woman, the Angel of Life, and other Poems*. Two years later he decided to take orders in the Established Church, and was in 1843 appointed minister of Percy Chapel, Charlotte Street, Fitzroy Square, which office he held till his death at Brighton. His preaching, which closely resembled his poetry, was much admired by connoisseurs. He was excessively vain, the type of the *cabotin piétiste*, and in his later years did a great deal for the welfare of Brompton Consumptive Hospital.

O   173

No extracts from his verse are complete without the comments of Macaulay, *judex, lictor, et exitium,* which are accordingly attached.

Marine Vignette

Oh! never did the dark-soul'd ATHEIST stand,
And watch the breakers boiling on the strand,
And, while Creation stagger'd at his nod,
Mock the dread presence of the mighty God!
We hear him in the wind-heaved ocean's roar,
Hurling her billowy crags upon the shore;
We hear him in the riot of the blast,
And shake, while rush the raving whirlwinds past.

THE OMNIPRESENCE OF THE DEITY.

["If Mr. Robert Montgomery's genius were not far too free and aspiring to be shackled by the rules of syntax, we should suppose that it is at the nod of the Atheist that Creation staggers. But Mr. Robert Montgomery's readers must take such grammar as they can get, and be thankful."]

A Request

YES! pause and think, within one fleeting hour
How vast a universe obeys Thy power;
Unseen, but felt, Thine interfused control
Works in each atom, and pervades the whole;
Expands the blossom, and erects the tree,
Conducts each vapour, and commands each sea,
Beams in each ray, bids whirlwinds be unfurl'd,
Unrolls the thunder, and upheaves a world.

IBID.

["No field-preacher surely ever carried his irreverent familiarity so far as to bid the Supreme Being stop and think on the importance of the interests which are under his care. The grotesque indecency of such an address throws into shade the subordinate absurdities of the passage, the unfurling of whirlwinds, the unrolling of thunder, and the upheaving of worlds."]

Fore and Aft

O DEATH! thou dauntless vanquisher of earth,
The Elements shrank blasted at thy birth!
Careering round the world like tempest wind,
Martyrs before, and victims strew'd behind;
Ages on ages cannot grapple thee,
Dragging the world into eternity!

IBID.

["If there be any one line in this passage about which we are more in the dark than about the rest, it is the fourth. What the difference may be between the victims and the martyrs, and why the martyrs are to lie before Death, and the victims behind him, are to us great mysteries."]

On the Revolution

AND here let Memory turn her tearful glance
On the dark horrors of tumultuous France,
When blood and blasphemy defiled her land,
And fierce Rebellion shook her savage hand.
Let the foul orgies of infuriate crime
Picture the raging havoc of that time,
When leagued Rebellion march'd to kindle man,
Fright in her rear, and Murder in her van.
And thou, sweet flower of Austria, slaughter'd Queen,
Who dropp'd no tear upon the dreadful scene,
When gush'd the life-blood from thine angel-form,
And martyr'd beauty perish'd in the storm,
Once worshipp'd paragon of all who saw,
Thy look obedience, and thy smile a law.

IBID.

["Whether Rebellion shakes her own hand, shakes the hand of Memory, or shakes the hand of France, or what any of these three metaphors mean, we know no more than we know what is the sense of the following passage. What is the distinction between the foul orgies and the raging havoc which the foul orgies are to picture? Why does Fright go behind Rebellion, and Murder before? Why should not Murder fall behind Fright? Or why should not all the three walk abreast? . . . 'Perish'd in the storm' means nothing at all; and 'thy look obedience' means the very reverse of what Mr. Robert Montgomery intends to say."]

CHARLES MACKAY (1814–89)

CHARLES MACKAY, a Scotsman educated at Brussels, entered journalism and became editor of the *Illustrated London News* in 1852. It was round about this time that the publication of a series of breezy lyrics—one of them was *Cheer, Boys, Cheer!* set to music by Henry Russell, which swept the country as thoroughly as *The Absent-Minded Beggar, Thora,* or *Ramona*—brought him considerable popularity and royalties. He was the New York special correspondent of *The Times* during the American Civil War, and his despatches on the Fenian movement increased his reputation. He collected and published (1867) *A Thousand and One Gems of English Poetry,* including some of his own.

The Earl and the Girl

[*The betrayal*]

WESTWOOD, sitting sadly by himself,
Read and re-read a letter just received
From his best friend, and comrade of his heart,
The Vicar.
        "My poor boy!" the father said,
"How will he bear it?—how shall I make known
This utter blight of his fast blossoming hopes?
The desecration of the holy shrine
Which he imagined in a woman's heart?
And she has yielded!—yielded to her aunt,
Her father and her brother—all her kin,
And given her hand to that superb old Earl—
Alas, poor Arthur!—hush! the victim comes!"

[*Arthur learns the news*——]

"Had any other name been signed but that,
I should have called him liar to his teeth!
But do not comfort me.   I'm sick at heart!
Where is *The Times*? no doubt 'tis blazoned there,
In the broad columns, 'Marriage in High Life.
The Earl Fitz-Neville and his youthful bride,
The daughter of Sir Thomas Arundel,
Left Erlwood Abbey yesterday for France.'"

[——*and, accompanied by his father, seeks oblivion in
foreign travel*]

They went to Naples, thence to Sicily,
And thence to Athens.   Arthur could not rest.
He thought he'd like to row upon the Nile,
And see the Pyramids; and so they went,
And rowed upon the Nile, and thought it dull;
And saw the Pyramids, and thought them small.
And next they tried the Desert—what of that?
It *was* a desert,—but in their degree,
Pall Mall, the Boulevards, and the Grand Canal,
Are they not deserts also, if the heart
Find not another heart in all their scope?

[*Deathbed of the superb old Earl*]

They took him home,
And plied the electric wire for speedy help,
And brought physicians from the capital,
Who came express by horses and by steam,
And issued bulletins from day to day.

A MAN'S HEART.

A Challenge

Come if you dare, reivers and raiders!
Come if you dare, to our beautiful shore;
Come if you dare, saucy invaders!
Many or few, you'll return nevermore.
One purpose shall fire us, one thought shall inspire us,
Each bullet we drive shall be true to a hair,
We'll give the full strength of you
Graves the full length of you,
Yes! every one of you, *Come if you dare!*

THE VOLUNTEERS

Only a Thought

'Twas only a passing thought, my love,
  Only a passing thought,
That came o'er my mind like a ray of the sun
  In the ripples of waters caught;
And it seemed to me, and I say to thee,
  That sorrow and shame and sin
Might disappear from our happy sphere,
  If we knew but to begin;
If we knew but how to profit
  By wisdom dearly bought:
'Twas only a passing thought, my love,
  Only a passing thought.

EDGAR ALLAN POE (1809–49)

WITH the fiery genius and smoky delirium of EDGAR ALLAN POE there went something which, had he concentrated on it to the exclusion of all the rest, would have secured him immediate fame and large sales with the English-speaking bourgeoisie; namely, an inexpensive rhetoric of a German kind, decorative, sentimental, completely null, expressed very often in the ballad form and pink-sugared with the most romantic names— Fortunato, Guy de Vere, Annabel, D'Elormie, Eulalie. Instead, he alarmed and confused the respectable reading public with his horrors and visions and spectres and Houses of Usher and murders in the Rue Morgue, and so died alone, wasted, drugged, and destitute, in a Baltimore hospital.

The instrument from which Poe could evoke such dooms was perfectly capable of producing notes from its upper register like the music of a tin whistle, the prattlings of a Haynes Bayly or the bleats of a Wordsworth. Of such a kind are the two opening stanzas of *For Annie*, which follow; a fastidious reproduction, one might almost say, of the entry of the district nurse, wilfully sympathetic, flustered, untying bonnet-strings, panting slightly. It is included in the *Oxford Book of English Verse*. The *Bridal Ballad* is in the best Bayly manner.

Poe constantly wrote far otherwise than this. It was, in consequence, some thirty years after his death that his puzzled countrymen at length decided to erect a monument to him.

Prone

THANK Heaven! the crisis—
  The danger is past
And the lingering illness
  Is over at last—
And the fever called "Living"
  Is conquer'd at last.

Sadly, I know,
　　I am shorn of my strength,
And no muscle I move
　　As I lie at full length—
But no matter—I feel
　　I am better at length.

　　　　　　　　　　　FOR ANNIE.

Bridal Ballad

THE ring is on my hand,
　　And the wreath is on my brow;
Satins and jewels grand
Are all at my command,
　　And I am happy now.

And my lord he loves me well;
　　But when first he breathed his vow,
I felt my bosom swell—
For the words rang as a knell,
And the voice seemed *his* who fell
In the battle down the dell,
　　And who is happy now.

But he spoke to reassure me,
　　And he kissed my pallid brow,
While a reverie came o'er me,
And to the churchyard bore me,
And I sighed to him before me,
Thinking him dead D'Elormie,
　　"Oh, I am happy now!"

And thus the words were spoken,
　　And thus the plighted vow;
And though my faith be broken,
And though my heart be broken,
Behold the golden token
　　That *proves* me happy now!

Would God I could awaken!
  For I dream I know not how,
And my soul is sorely shaken
Lest an evil step be taken—
Lest the dead who is forsaken
  May not be happy now.

Eulalie

I DWELT alone
  In a world of moan,
    And my soul was a stagnant tide,
Till the fair and gentle Eulalie became my blushing
    bride—
Till the yellow-haired young Eulalie became my smiling
    bride.

    Ah less—less bright
    The stars of the night
  Than the eyes of the radiant girl!
    And never a flake
    That the vapour can make
  With the moon-tints of purple and pearl,
Can vie with the modest Eulalie's most unregarded curl—
Can compare with the bright-eyed Eulalie's most humble
    and careless curl.

    Now Doubt—now Pain
    Come never again,
  For her soul gives me sigh for sigh,
    And all the day long
    Shines bright and strong
  Astartè within the sky,
While ever to her dear Eulalie upturns her matron eye—
While ever to her young Eulalie upturns her violet eye.

THOMAS HOLLEY CHIVERS (*fl.* 1840)

"Poe," observes Bayard Taylor, "finished the ruin of him which Shelley began." Taylor is referring to Poe's contemporary Thomas Holley Chivers, by profession a medical man in Georgia but by calling a poet—for he published six volumes of verse.

Certain definite influences, indeed, are perceptible in Chivers's verse; but Rosalie Lee—her names betray a slight tone-deafness in her creator—is more decorative than her sister Annabel, more anthosmial, more hyaline, and Lily Adair driving her fiery chariot is a healthier and more womanly open-air Nordic type than any of Poe's pallid heroines. One sees the poet hastily removing his tall hat and waving it in farewell as Miss Adair, star-crowned, sweeps through the upper air, like Elijah, to Heaven. "Well, good-bye, Mr. Chivers!"

And what is a reboantic Norn?

Miss Adair

The Apollo Belvidere was adorning
   The chamber where Eulalie lay,
While Aurora, the Rose of the Morning,
   Smiled full in the face of the Day.
All around stood the beautiful Graces
   Bathing Venus—some combing her hair—
While she lay in her husband's embraces
   A-moulding my Lily Adair—
   Of my fawn-like Lily Adair—
   Of my dove-like Lily Adair—
   Of my beautiful, dutiful Lily Adair. . . .

Where the opaline Swan circled, singing,
   With her eider-down Cygnets at noon,

In the tall jasper Reeds that were springing
　　From the marge of the crystal Lagoon—
Rich Canticles, clarion-like, golden,
　　Such as only true love can declare,
Like an Archangel's voice in times olden—
　　I went with my Lily Adair—
　　With my lamb-like Lily Adair—
　　With my saint-like Lily Adair—
　　With my beautiful, dutiful Lily Adair. . . .

From her Paradise Isles in the ocean
　　To the beautiful City of On,
By the mellifluent rivers of Goschen,
　　My beautiful Lily is gone!
In her Chariot of Fire translated,
　　Like Elijah she passed through the air,
To the City of God, golden-gated—
　　The Home of my Lily Adair—
　　Of my star-crowned Lily Adair—
　　Of my God-loved Lily Adair—
　　Of my beautiful, dutiful Lily Adair.

Eonchs of Ruby.

Miss Lee

Many mellow Cydonian suckets,
　　Sweet apples, anthosmial, divine,
From the ruby-rimmed beryline buckets,
　　Star-gemmed, lily-shaped, hyaline:
Like the sweet golden goblet found growing
　　On the wild emerald cucumber-tree,
Rich, brilliant, like chrysoprase glowing,
　　Was my beautiful Rosalie Lee.

Rosalie Lee.

A Call

In the music of the morns,
Blown through Conchimarian horns,
Down the dark vistas of the reboantic Norns,
To the Genius of Eternity,
Crying: "Come to me! Come to me!"

THE POET'S VOCATION.

From "*The Vigil of Aiden*"

In the Rosy Bowers of Aiden
With her ruby lips love-laden
Dwelt the mild, the modest maiden
   Whom Politian calls Lenore.
As the churches, with their whiteness
Clothe the earth with their uprightness,
Clothes she now his soul with brightness,
   Breathing out her heart's love-lore;
For her lily limbs so tender,
Like the moon in her own splendor
Seemed all earthly things to render
   Bright as Eden was of yore.

Then he cried out broken-hearted,
In this desert world deserted,
Though she had not yet departed,
"Are we not to meet, dear maiden!
In the Rosy Bowers of Aiden,
   As we did in days of yore?"
And that modest, mild, sweet maiden,
In the Rosy Bowers of Aiden,
With her lily-lips love-laden
   Answered, "Yes! forevermore!"
And the old-time Tower of Aiden
   Echoed, "Yes! forevermore!" . . .

Then her mother cried, "My daughter!"
As from earth the angels caught her,
She had passed the Stygian water
    On the Asphodelian shore! . . .

As the lips of that damned Demon,
Like the Syren to the seamen,
With the voice of his dear Leman
    Answered, "Never—nevermore!" . .

Through the luminiferous Gihon,
To the Golden City high on
High Eternity's Mount Zion,
    God built in the Days of Yore—
To the Golden Land of Goschen,
Far beyond Time's upper ocean,
Where, beholding our devotion,
    Float the argent orbs all o'er—
To Avillon's happy Valley,
Where the breezes ever dally
With the roses in each alley—
    There to rest forevermore.

ELIZABETH BARRETT BROWNING (1809–61)

THE serene and fruitful life of ELIZABETH BARRETT BROWNING admits of no extended survey here. At the age of twelve, in the quiet of Hope End, Herefordshire, her father's country house, with its tasteful Moorish *décor*, she wrote an epic on Marathon, in four books; at seventeen her girlish fancy had already flowered in an Essay on Mind. *Prometheus* followed at twenty-six; and in 1843 she met Browning, whom according to one reading she describes in a notable passage as a pomegranate which, if cut deep down the middle, shows a heart within blood-tinctured of a veined humanity. Mr. Browning, whose complexion was rosy, took no umbrage at this. The marriage followed in 1846, and was uniformly idyllic. Hawthorne, who stayed with the Brownings at Casa Guidi, their Florentine home, is but one of their enraptured visitors who have recorded it: through the open windows of the drawing-room at Casa Guidi, crowded with a thousand pretty and tasteful knick-knacks, could be heard at evening the singing of Vespers at Santa Felice opposite, where the natives were at their quaint but picturesque devotions. It was at this period that a bustling transatlantic visitor described Mrs. Browning as "a soul of fire enclosed in a shell of pearl."

The following stanzas from *Lady Geraldine's Courtship* display a tribute to the Peerage in a style which has since lapsed. Now that the Peerage is composed of every class without social distinctions a new poet may yet arise even more enthusiastic than Mrs. Browning.

Snoblesse Oblige

THERE's a lady—an earl's daughter; she is proud and she is noble,
And she treads the crimson carpet, and she breathes the perfumed air;

And a kingly blood sends glances up her princely eye to
   trouble,
And the shadow of a monarch's crown is softened in her
   hair.

She has halls and she has castles, and the resonant
   steam-eagles
Follow far on the direction of her little dove-like hand—
Trailing on a thundrous vapour underneath the starry
   vigils,
So to mark upon the blasted heaven the measure of
   her land. . . .

Many vassals bow before her, as her chariot sweeps their
   doorways;
She hath blest their little children,—as a priest or queen
   were she!
Far too tender, or too cruel far, her smile upon the poor
   was,
For I thought it was the same smile, which she used to
   smile on *me*.

She has voters in the Commons, she has lovers in the
   palace—
And of all the fair court-ladies, few have jewels half so
   fine:
Even the prince has named her beauty, 'twixt the red
   wine and the chalice:
Oh, and what was *I* to love her? my beloved, my
   Geraldine!

LADY GERALDINE'S COURTSHIP.

HENRY WADSWORTH LONGFELLOW

(1807–82)

THE compilers, while holding stubbornly that a man who can produce strains of music like

> "I remember the black wharves and the slips,
>   And the sea-tides tossing free;
> And Spanish sailors with bearded lips,
> And the beauty and mystery of the ships,
>   And the magic of the sea,"

with its far-off refrain from an old Lapland song:

> "A boy's will is the wind's will,
> And the thoughts of youth are long, long thoughts,"

is a poet absolute, displayed, and regardant, in the Chief, the Pale, and the Quarter Fess, have held themselves bound in reason and honour to include in this book one of HENRY WADSWORTH LONGFELLOW's more enduringly popular pieces of verse.

A bitter controversy has raged round the young man's cry of "*Excelsior!*" One school of philologists holds that he meant to cry "*Excelsius!*" the comparative of the adverb *excelsè*, but that what with the late hour and the severe Alpine cold and (as Miss Beatrice Lillie would say) what with this and what with that, he confused it with the comparative of the adjective or past participle *excelsus*. Arrayed in opposition is a school which insists that the banner with a strange device and the young man's odd behaviour were deliberately designed by Longfellow, the seer, to foreshadow the more striking developments of American Publicity, and that "*Excelsior!*" therefore is to be regarded as perfectly good Big Business Latin.

To this controversy the compilers do not wish to contribute. They would merely point out, before passing on, that the poet's suggestion that village maidens in Switzerland are in the habit of inviting complete strangers to lay their heads on their virgin breasts has been strongly censured by many who consider it an unwarrantable slur on the morals of a British Dependency.

Excelsior

THE shades of night were falling fast,
As through an Alpine village passed
A youth, who bore, 'mid snow and ice,
A banner with the strange device,
      Excelsior!

His brow was sad; his eye beneath
Flashed like a falchion from its sheath,
And like a silver clarion rung
The accents of that unknown tongue,
      Excelsior!

In happy homes he saw the light
Of household fires gleam warm and bright;
Above, the spectral glaciers shone,
And from his lips escaped a groan,
      Excelsior!

"Try not the Pass!" the old man said;
"Dark lowers the tempest overhead,
The roaring torrent is deep and wide!"
And loud that clarion voice replied,
      Excelsior!

"O stay," the maiden said, "and rest
Thy weary head upon this breast!"
A tear stood in his bright blue eye,
But still he answered, with a sigh,
      Excelsior!

"Beware the pine-tree's withered branch!
Beware the awful avalanche!"
This was the peasant's last Good-night.
A voice replied, far up the height,
     Excelsior!

At break of day, as heavenward
The pious monks of Saint Bernard
Uttered the oft-repeated prayer,
A voice cried through the startled air,
     Excelsior!

A traveller, by the faithful hound,
Half-buried in the snow was found,
Still grasping in his hands of ice
That banner with the strange device,
     Excelsior!

There in the twilight cold and grey,
Lifeless, but beautiful, he lay,
And from the sky, serene and far,
A voice fell, like a falling star,
     Excelsior!

T. BAKER (*fl.* 1837-57)

LITTLE or no discovery has rewarded diligent research into the career of T. BAKER, except the fact that he was inexhaustibly impressed by the powers of steam. He himself records in verse that in 1837 he crossed, in some solemnity, to Cork by the steam-packet, and was scandalised by the irreligious behaviour of some Irish passengers who passed the voyage in laughter and light-mindedness, in the manner of their race. One may well believe that T. Baker on this occasion shared the just sentiments of Mr. King in Mr. Kipling's story: "I tell you, Gillett, if the Romans had dealt faithfully with the Celt, *ab initio*, this would never have happened."

We may assume that T. Baker was at this moment at least twenty years old. He would therefore have been born about 1817, and by 1837 was probably beginning to be known in Sydenham as "the Mr. Baker who is fond of steam." His views on the Irish question favoured sterner repressive measures. A few years later came the *coup de foudre*: he became a lover of the Great Western Railway, and in 1857 at length published *The Steam-Engine ; or, the Power of Flame, an Original Poem, in Ten Cantos, by T. Baker* (London, J. S. Hodson, Portugal Street, Lincoln's Inn); a poem of 200 pages (with lyrics) which, the author points out in his preface, "not only refers to the great achievements of the Flame-Powers, but also to the almost divine aspirations of their Foster-Sires; who, in a truly Christian spirit, sought to aggrandise and elevate the human race." He was among the first to observe that the Great Western track is so planned that two engines running on separate parallel rails may meet and pass, but can never crash into each other. The fate of the eminent financier and politician Mr. Huskisson, who fell on the line and was run over, did not shake T. Baker's belief in the power of Flame, and—unlike Alfred, Lord Tennyson—he was too reverently familiar with his idol to fall into the monstrous error of believing the wheels to run in grooves. He may have married about 1840. The honeymoon was doubtless spent at Paddington.

The Irish potato famine of 1846 drew no recorded comment from him; but his pursed lips, cold blue eye, dry cough, and deliberate changing of the subject were probably eloquent enough. The death of George Stephenson in 1848 must have moved him deeply, and although no threnody from his pen is preserved, it is likely that he composed several, and a careful probing of the archives of the Great Western Railway might bring these to light.

Not much more can be said of T. Baker, and even with all the available evidence this appreciation has already assumed the appearance of a string of hypotheses closely resembling Sir Sidney Lee's *Life of Shakespeare*. He may have lived to vote against Mr. Gladstone's iniquitous Home Rule proposals. His old age may have been mellowed by the success of a son, George Stephenson Rocket Baker, as an engine-driver. Nothing is known. Yet it can be claimed for T. Baker that he is the progenitor of the Great Western Railway School of English Verse, and his contemporary, Mr. Close, some of whose enthusiasm is likewise represented in this book, is not a whit more secure than he in the solemn realisation that Millennium has arrived.

It is only necessary to add that the lines in the first extract:

> "His frame was made to emulate the duck,
>   Webb'd feet had he, in Ocean's brine to play,"

refer not to Lord Stanhope (as might appear from a hasty first reading) but to the paddle-steamer of his Lordship's patronage. "His Lordship's feet and frame were most agreeably formed, and perfectly adapted to meet every obligation of the high rank and privilege to which it pleases God to call an English nobleman." [1]

Lord Stanhope's Steamer

Lord Stanhope hit upon a novel plan
Of bringing forth this vast Leviathan
(This notion first Genevois' genius struck);
His frame was made to emulate the duck;

[1] Extract from a communication of Mr. Banks, his Lordship's butler, to *The Times*, January 6, 1858.

Webb'd feet had he, in Ocean's brine to play;
With whale-like might he whirl'd aloft the spray;
But made with all this splash but little speed;
Alas! the duck was doom'd not to succeed!

THE STEAM-ENGINE, CANTO IV.

On The Cork Packet, 1837

THE breeze grew strong, the waves show'd crests of foam,
While sickness made our landsmen sigh for home.
This scene I won't describe.—I hasten'd soon,
With many others, to the grand saloon.
Tourists there were, and trav'llers mercantile,
In groups, too, were the sons of Erin's Isle;
All gay, her youthful beaux were shining forth,
Had seen the greatest city upon earth;
While from their converse (any one could guess),
Of feasts and revelry to wild excess,
Their grov'lling minds had moved them but to see
Its gaudy side, and have what's called a spree.
Mere sensualists! such, I regret to find,
Is the low taste in most of humankind,
That e'en Augusta's high-wrought works of art
Can no ennobling thoughts to them impart!

IBID., CANTO VI.

Great Western Days

TRIUMPHANT was the burst of rapt'rous joy
That hail'd our HERO's [1] young victorious BOY,
The great opponent of both time and space,
Brave young ACHILLES,[2] chief of all his race,
When in the pride of his paternal strength,
With splendid train of more than civic length,

[1] Steam.

[2] The early Great Western locomotives were named from the Iliad.

He first by Thames in all his pomp was seen,
His triumph graced by Britain's virtuous Queen,
By prince, by senators, and lords of state,
With minds replete with skill to legislate,
Journeying for pleasure, or their wish'd-for home,
Or regal Windsor's high embattled dome;
While merchant, agriculturist, alderman,
And every grade, from peer to artizan,
The knowing sage, the clown devoid of thought,
By casual conflux there together brought,
Were borne with more than e'en the fabled speed
Of famed Arabian prophet's flying steed. . . .
Ajax pursues, but not his friend to gain,
An equal distance still divides each train;
Hector is met by both, their speed at par,
Short time for greeting, none at all for war.

IBID., CANTO IX.

The Death of Huskisson

THE trains are stopp'd, the MIGHTY CHIEFS OF FLAME
To quench their thirst the crystal water claim;
While from their post the great in crowds alight,
When, by a line-train, in its hasty flight,
Through striving to avoid it, Huskisson
By unforeseen mischance was over-run.
That stroke, alas! was death in shortest time;
Thus fell the great financier in his prime!
This fatal chance not only caused delay,
But damped the joy that erst had crown'd the day.

IBID., CANTO X.

Roses All the Way

AT length the Steam-Chiefs with replenish'd force
To Manchester pursued their pageant course;
A grand reception there secure they found;
And though acclaim still made the air resound,

The blithe response was clogg'd with grief's alloy,
The fate of Huskisson still chill'd their joy.
The mutual greetings and the banquet o'er,
The Steam-Chiefs, in procession as before,
With equal pomp and eight-fold gorgeous train,
Forthwith returned to Liverpool again:
While still the eager crowds, we scarce need say,
Their progress hail'd with plaudits all the way.
Now in conclusion, 'twould be vain to tell,
How high at Liverpool was rapture's swell!
How rich the banquet and how choice the wines,
Where thus in state the mighty Arthur dines!
While eloquence, like the occasion, rare,
May be inferr'd, since Peel and Brougham were there!

IBID.

The Railway Boom, 1845

NEW schemes, not even dream'd of once before,
Were lauded loudly, puff'd off even more
Than e'en the grand trunk-system that imparts
Connection to our chief commercial marts.
Nor was this MANIA, this eccentric roar,
Confined alone within Britannia's shore;
It made its way at that eventful time
To every land without respect to clime.
Vast were the schemes that now came forth in France,
Though not so wont in Britain's wake t' advance.
Europe was smitten to the very core,
And thence the MANIA raged from shore to shore:
East and West Indies groan'd 'neath the disease,
Its virulence uncheck'd by rolling seas.
Nay, e'en Van Diemen's Land and New South Wales
Determined, like the rest, to have their rails.

IBID.

A Lesson for the Proud

THE scheme is tried; and shall it prosper too?
Yes; what can't STEAM and gold united do?
Near the commencement of Victoria's reign,
Both SEA-CHIEFS started on th' Atlantic main;
While all the merchantmen they met or pass'd,
Long looks of wonder on the HEROES cast;
Their proud, majestic march, their stately air,
Their god-like prowess, and their length of car,
Made gazers all, with great reluctance, see
Their own comparative nonentity.

IBID., CANTO VII.

Vision

of the World, regenerated by the Gospel and the Power of Steam

I DREAM'D I walk'd, in raptures high,
   Through realms of sunny clime,
Not of this earth; they seem'd to lie
   Beyond the bourne of time.

Nor did they seem all heav'nly fair,
   But happy fields between
This lowly earth of vexing care
   And the celestial scene. . . .

No labour long and hard oppress'd
   The happy human race,
Save pleasing tasks with bracing rest,
   In this exalted place.

No beast, throughout its breadth and length,
   Was e'er compell'd to toil;
For POWERS of superhuman strength
   Gave culture to the soil.

The chariots here, in gorgeous train,
  Sped swift in pageant tours;
And vessels on the rolling main,
  Moved by these MIGHTY POWERS. ....

I'd seen these god-like POWERS before
  On this our lowly earth;
Was present at th' auspicious hour,
  When they received their birth:

Yet here I miss'd the vexing cares,
  The avarice and pride,
The loud contentions, angry jars,
  Which man from man divide.

My wonder deep one standing near
  At once deign'd to explain;
"Behold," he said, "the destined sphere
  Of GREAT MESSIAH's reign!

"HE slavish toil and care destroy'd,
  By aid of THESE VAST POWERS;
While bliss, like Eden's, is enjoy'd
  In this bright land of ours!

"And strangled by HIS mighty hold
  Are vice and sin and woe;
As holy prophets had foretold
  Some thousand years ago!"

Th' advancing day's tumultuous noise
  My happy slumber broke;
From raptures of celestial joys,
  To real scenes I woke;

Not without hopes the time would come.
  When earth would be renew'd,
With all such glories in their bloom,
  As I in vision view'd!

IBID., CANTO IX.

ELIZA COOK (1818–89)

Miss Cook, a native of London, entered the service of the Muses before the age of fifteen. Her first considerable poem, *I'm Afloat!* attracted favourable criticism, the *Athenæum* remarking on the buoyancy of the author's style. *Lays of a Wild Harp* followed, and in 1836 the publication in the *Weekly Dispatch* of *The Old Arm-Chair*, over the initials "E. C.," was something of a literary event. Public appreciation, shared by the Highest Quarters, at length forced the new poet to emerge from concealment, and (says the *Dictionary of National Biography*) "the result was a handsome pecuniary acknowledgment and a regular engagement to subscribe [contribute?] to the paper." In 1838 appeared *Melaia, and other Poems*; fresh editions were called for in 1840, in 1845; a New York edition was published in 1844. The theme of *Melaia*, indeed, was one to stir the imaginations of a free, proud, and imperial race; it was set in a rich but not voluptuous Oriental atmosphere, and described the attachment of a faithful dog to its master. Whether or not (as was eagerly debated in the *Quarterly Review* and elsewhere by several clergymen and others) the dog was actually a Retriever or not seems to us now irrelevant and in no way pertinent to the scope of the poem.

In 1849 there was issued *Eliza Cook's Journal*, a periodical of an interesting but moral character. It ceased to appear in 1854; the poem *I'm Sunk!* which some critics attach to this moment, is probably the work of the pseudo-Cook, as Dr. Rottmacher has sufficiently proved (*Englands Selbstbesinnung durch Eliza Cook*, Leipsic, 1859; *Der Conjunctiv bei Eliza*, 1860; *Beiträge zum Cookproblem*, 1862). She received a Civil List pension of one hundred pounds in 1863 and died at Wimbledon.

Her poetry, says her biographer, appealed very strongly to the middle classes—like *Oliver Cromwell*, that modern drama. She was a friend of Longfellow, and is believed to have inspired, directly or indirectly, the more metaphysical portions of *The*

Village Blacksmith. And if the reader gains from the examples of her verse which follow a fixed impression that she was invariably a rather soft and silly spinster lady, the compilers recommend the study—elsewhere—of her *Song of the Worm*, an exercise in the *macabre* which is pure Holbein.

Trombone Solo

THERE'S a land that bears a world-known name,
    Though it is but a little spot;
I say 'tis first on the scroll of Fame,
    And who shall say it is not?
Of the deathless ones who shine and live
    In Arms, in Arts, or Song,
The brightest the whole wide world can give
    To that little land belong.
'Tis the star of earth, deny it who can;
The island home of an Englishman.

There's a flag that waves o'er every sea,
    No matter when or where;
And to treat that flag as aught but the free
    Is more than the strongest dare.
For the lion-spirits that tread the deck
    Have carried the palm of the brave;
And that flag *may* sink with a shot-torn wreck,
    But never float over a slave.
Its honour is stainless, deny it who can;
And this is the flag of an Englishman.

There's a heart that leaps with burning glow,
    The wronged and the weak to defend;
And strikes as soon for a trampled foe,
    As it does for a soul-bound friend.
It nurtures a deep and honest love;
    It glows with faith and pride;

And yearns with the fondness of a dove,
  To the light of its own fireside.
'Tis a rich, rough gem, deny it who can;
And this is the heart of an Englishman.

The Briton may traverse the pole or the zone,
  And boldly claim his right;
For he calls such a vast domain his own,
  That the sun never sets on his might.
Let the haughty stranger seek to know
  The place of his home and birth;
And a flush will pour from cheek to brow,
  While he tells his native earth.
For a glorious charter, deny it who can,
Is breathed in the words, "I'm an Englishman."

THE ENGLISHMAN.

Live and Let Live

THERE is room in the world for more pleasure,
  If Man would but learn to be just;
And regret when his fellow-man's measure
  Runs over with tear-drops and dust.
We were sent here to help one another,
  And he who neglects the behest
Disgraces the milk of his mother,
  And spreadeth Love's pall o'er his breast.
And the spirit that covets unduly,
  Holds sin that 'tis hard to forgive;
For Religion ne'er preaches more truly
  Than when she says, "Live and let live."

Becalmed in the Tropics

MANY a lip is gaping for drink,
  And madly calling for rain;
And some hot brains are beginning to think
  Of a messmate's opened vein.

SONG OF THE SEA-WEED.

A Thought

THERE'S a mission, no doubt, for the mole in the dust,
   As there is for the charger, with nostrils of pride;
The sloth and the newt have their places of trust,
   And the agents are needed, for God has supplied.
                    THERE IS NOTHING IN VAIN.

From "The Old Arm-Chair"

I LOVE it, I love it; and who shall dare
To chide me for loving that old Arm-chair?
I've treasured it long as a sainted prize;
I've bedewed it with tears, and embalmed it with sighs.
'Tis bound by a thousand bands to my heart;
Not a tie will break, not a link will start.
Would ye learn the spell?—a mother sat there;
And a sacred thing is that old Arm-chair.

Entry of the Marines

OLD England! thy name shall yet warrant thy fame,
   If the brow of the foeman should scowl;
Let the Lion be stirred by too daring a word,
   And beware of his echoing growl.
We have still the same breed of the man and the steed
   That wore nobly our Waterloo wreath;
We have more of the blood that formed Inkerman's flood,
   When it poured in the whirlpool of Death;
And the foeman will find neither coward nor slave
'Neath the Red Cross of England—the Flag of the Brave.

We have jackets of blue, still as dauntless and true
   As the tars that our Nelson led on;
Give them room on the main, and they'll show us again
   How the Nile and Trafalgar were won.
Let a ball show its teeth, let a blade leave its sheath,
   To defy the proud strength of our might,

We have iron-mouthed guns, we have steel-hearted sons,
    That will prove how the Britons can fight.
Our ships and our sailors are kings of the wave,
'Neath the Red Cross of England—the Flag of the Brave.

Though a tear might arise in our women's bright eyes,
    And a sob check the fearful "Good-bye,"
Yet these women would send lover, brother or friend,
    To the war-field, to conquer or die!
Let the challenge be flung from the braggart's bold
        tongue,
    And that challenge will fiercely be met;
And our banner unfurled shall proclaim to the world
    That "there's life in the old dog yet."
Hurrah! for the men on the land or the wave,
'Neath the Red Cross of England—the Flag of the Brave.

THE RED CROSS OF ENGLAND.

A Thought

THE sweet and merry sunshine makes the very church-
    yard fair;
We half forget the yellow bones, while yellow flowers
    are there;
And while the summer beams are thrown upon the
    osiered heap,
We tread with lingering footsteps where our "rude fore-
    fathers sleep."
The hemlock does not seem so rank—the willow is not
    dull;
The rich flood lights the coffin nail and burnishes the
    skull.
Oh! the sweet and merry sunshine is a pleasant thing to
    see,
Though it plays upon a grave-stone through the gloomy
    cypress tree.

SUNSHINE.

SAMUEL CARTER (*fl.* 1848–51)

A REVIEW in *Tait's Edinburgh Magazine* reveals the truth concerning SAMUEL CARTER, and why he became a poet. Mr. Carter published his bulky *Midnight Effusions* in 1848, explaining in the preface that he was a young briefless barrister who had taken to verse "at the dead hour of night, in the solitude of my own chamber," and arguing that this indulgence left him no less fit for "the stirring duties of an advocate, or the calmer business of a legal adviser," than if he had spent his nights in the billiard-room, the tavern, or the theatre. A knotty point.

Mr. Carter's gift for stirring the emotions is proved by the following extract from his poetic drama, *The Avenger, a Metrical Tale* (1851). The behaviour of the Italian Brigand is typical of his odious kind, and we rejoice with the nurse at the cheering hint, conveyed in the last couplet, of his approaching end. And the poet's tribute to the metropolitan sewage system is at once just, finely expressed, and almost modern in its choice of theme.

Incident in Italy

[The Brigand destroys a maiden :]

> THE monster seized the shrieking girl,
> Around her throat his fingers met,
> And swept her down with giant hand
> The frightful opening at his feet.

[Her sister arrives, and spectators think of interfering :]

> And rushing on with frantic cries,
> Horror and madness in her eyes,
> Rosa was seen, towards the cave
> Just made her living sister's grave.

Those who looked on half stupefied
At the enormous homicide,
Thinking she aimed herself to throw
Into the dreadful pit below,
Stepped forth to intercept her course,
But just before the wretch she neared
She fell with some degree of force,
And for a moment stunned appeared.

With frantic grief she tore her hair,
The kerchief round her bosom bound,
And dashed her head against the ground;
Then rising up with rapid speed
While neck, and ears, and forehead bleed,
She struggled vainly to address
The miscreant, who from the press
Still kept aloof. . . .

[*But the march of events is too quick for them :*]

He seized her in his arms to fling
Her down the grave her sister found.—
The suddenness of this attack
So paralysed each looker on,
That taken by it quite aback
They stand as if transformed to stone,
And see, astonished and amazed,
The poor girl with the murderer
Struggle for life—and as they gazed
Made no attempt to aid or stir.

[*Rosa does her best unaided :*]

And once when groping for his knife
To terminate that way the strife,
Her efforts to preserve her life
Became so great as almost drew
The villain to destruction too.

Q

[The miscreant is overpowered and put to bed :]

So stunned, surrounded and beset,
The surgeon struggled hard to see
His patient, or at least to get
Some signs of his proximity:
At length they opened up a way
To where a man extended, lay,
Presenting an appalling sight
Seen dimly through the chequered light. . . .
For swelling, high amid the clothes,
The body, like a mountain rose
That scarce the head was seen;
While from below the feet protrude
(Like Satan "stretching many a rood"
So giant-like I ween.)—
And on those large and naked feet
A pair of antique spurs were placed,
Which fastened o'er the instep meet,
With many-coloured latchets graced.

[The surgeon enquires later:]

"Since when he has," (replied the nurse,)
"Been going on from bad to worse."

THE AVENGER.

The Passing of Arthur

[The Magistrate, loq. :]

You have confessed, and by a recent Act,
The 80 chapter, 13 George the Third,
The penalties, thereto attached, incurred,
Which says, if any in the night should dare,
With dog, or net, or gun, to kill a hare,
Between the hours of seven and six a.m.,
A magistrate may lawfully condemn

To pay a fine of Twenty Pounds, and we
Inflict upon you the full penalty;
And if you make default, or goods should fail,
Three months' confinement in the common jail.

ARTHUR MERVYN;
A TALE OF SOCIAL GRIEVANCES.

Pæan

MAGNIFICENT, too, is the system of drains,
Exceeding the far-spoken wonders of old:
So lengthen'd and vast in its branches and chains,
That labyrinths pass like a tale that is told:
The sewers gigantic, like multiplied veins,
Beneath the whole city their windings unfold,
Disgorging the source of plagues, scourges, and pains,
Which visit those cities to cleanliness cold.
Well did the ancient proverb lay down this important
      text,
That cleanliness for human weal to godliness is next.

LONDON.

MARTIN FARQUHAR TUPPER (1810-89)

THE reputation of MARTIN TUPPER was sufficiently considerable during the Victorian era to afford the compilers a mild glow of complacency in summoning it now from neglect. Indeed, it is impossible to fight long against the atmosphere of cosy, rosy complacency in which Mr. Tupper is enveloped. At Oxford he defeated his fellow-undergraduate William Ewart Gladstone for the Burton theological essay prize. On coming down he was called to the Bar, but forbore to practise. In 1838 the first series of *Proverbial Philosophy* appeared, and after an initial failure—even in America—soared into success. By 1876 it had been expanded into four series and the earlier volumes had run into sixty editions. An illustrated quarto edition was published as late as 1881. It has always been accounted poetry.

Mr. Tupper's worth was duly recognised. In 1844 he received the Prussian Gold Medal for Science and Art by the favour of Bunsen. Oxford, ever zealous in honouring letters, made him a D.C.L. in 1847, one year after he had become an F.R.S. In 1851 and 1876 his American admirers flocked to welcome him in their midst. In 1873, having suffered a financial set-back, he was granted a Civil List pension of £120. Ten years later the British Nation uprose as one man and presented him with a public testimonial. Nor was this all, for he had admirers in the bosom of the R—y—l F—m—ly itself, and during the Prince Consort's time was often to be seen at Court, in Queen Anne Court costume, paying mellifluous homage.

His other poetical works are *War Ballads* (1854), *Rifle Ballads* (1859), and *Protestant Ballads* (1874); he also wrote an autobiography in prose and a *Jubilate* in honour of Queen Victoria, whose approval was so gratifying. He was a vain, bland, naïve personage, and his success enabled him to withstand without flinching or sourness the savagery of critics like *Fraser's* and the gibes of parodists like Calverley, Cuthbert

208

Bede, and W. S. Gilbert, whose butt he remained. The Portrait of a Victorian Author which follows may be taken as a slightly idealised view of (among others) Mr. Tupper himself, but the reading, favoured by some scholars, which interpolates after the opening couplet this:

"A faint smile of conscious rectitude hypheneth his whiskers;
    His left hand shroudeth itself in his bosom; with his right he
        fingereth a royalty-statement,"

is probably spurious.

Portrait of a Victorian Author

YEA: how dignified, and worthy, full of privilege and
    happiness,
Standeth in majestic independence the self-ennobled
    Author!
For God hath blessed him with a mind, and cherished it
    in tenderness and purity,
Hath taught it in the whisperings of wisdom, and added
    all the riches of content:
Therefore, leaning on his God, a pensioner for soul and
    body,
His spirit is the subject of none other, calling no man
    Master.
His hopes are mighty and eternal, scorning small
    ambitions:
He hideth from the pettiness of praise, and pitieth the
    feebleness of envy.
If he meet honours, well; it may be his humility to take
    them:
If he be rebuked, better; his veriest enemy shall teach
    him.
For the master-mind hath a birthright of eminence; his
    cradle is an eagle's eyrie:
Need but to wait till his wings are grown, and Genius
    soareth to the sun:

To creeping things upon the mountain leaveth he the
  gradual ascent,
Resting his swiftness on the summit only for a higher
  flight.
Glad in clear good-conscience, lightly doth he look for
  commendation;
What, if the prophet lacketh honour? for he can spare
  that praise:
The honest giant careth not to be patted on the back by
  pigmies:
Flatter greatness, he brooketh it good-humouredly:
  blame him,—thou tiltest at a pyramid:
Yet, just censure of the good never can he hear without
  contrition;
Neither would he miss one wise man's praise, for scarce
  is that jewel and costly:
Only for the herd of common minds, and the vulgar
  trumpetings of fame,
If aught he heedeth in the matter, his honour is sought
  in their neglect.
Slender is the marvel, and little is the glory, when round
  his luscious fruits
The worm and the wasp and the multitude of flies are
  gathered as to banquet;
Fashion's freak, and the critical sting, and the flood of
  flatteries he scorneth;
Cheerfully asking of the crowd the favour to forget him:
The while his blooming fruits ripen in richer fragrance,
A feast for the few,—and the many yet unborn,—who
  still shall love their savour.

PROVERBIAL PHILOSOPHY, 2ND SERIES.

The Marriage Market

WHEN thou choosest a wife, think not only of thyself,
But of those God may give thee of her, that they reproach
  thee not for their being:

See that He hath given her health, lest thou lose her
early and weep:
See that she springeth of a wholesome stock, that thy
little ones perish not before thee:
For many a fair skin hath covered a mining disease,
And many a laughing cheek been bright with the glare
of madness.
Mark the converse of one thou lovest, that it be simple
and sincere;
For an artful or false woman shall set thy pillow with
thorns. . . .
Hath she wisdom? it is precious, but beware that thou
exceed;
For woman must be subject, and the true mastery is of
the mind.
Be joined to thine equal in rank, or the foot of pride will
kick at thee;
And look not only for riches, lest thou be mated with
misery:
Marry not without means; for so shouldst thou tempt
Providence;
But wait not for more than enough; for marriage is the
DUTY of most men:
Grievous indeed must be the burden that shall outweigh
innocence and health,
And a well-assorted marriage hath not many cares. . . .
If ye are blessed with children, ye have a fearful pleasure,
A deeper care and a higher joy, and the range of your
existence is widened:
If God in wisdom refuse them, thank Him for an unknown
mercy:
For how can ye tell if they might be a blessing or a curse?
Yet ye may pray, like Hannah, simply dependent on his
will:
Resignation sweeteneth the cup, but impatience dasheth
it with vinegar.

IBID., IST SERIES.

The Poor Relation ; or, Pious Hope Frustrated

I saw the humble relation that tended the peevishness of
    wealth,
And ministered, with kind hand, to the wailings of disease
    and discontent:
I noted how watchfulness and care were feeding on the
    marrow of her youth,
How heavy was the yoke of dependence, loaded by petty
    tyranny;
Yet I heard the frequent suggestion,—It can be but a
    little longer,
Patience and mute submission shall one day reap a
    rich reward.
So, tacitly enduring much, waited that humble friend,
Putting off the lover of her youth until the dawn of
    wealth:
And it came, that day of release, and the freed heart
    could not sorrow,
For now were the years of promise to yield their golden
    harvest:
Hope, so long deferred, sickly sparkled in her eye,
The miserable past was forgotten, as she looked for the
    happier future,
And she checked, as unworthy and ungrateful, the dark
    suspicious thought
That perchance her right had been safer, if not left alone
    with honour:
But, alas, the sad knowledge soon came, that her stern
    task-master's will
Hath rewarded her toil with a jibe, her patience with
    utter destitution!—
Shall not the scourge of justice lash that cruel coward,
Who mingled the gall of ingratitude with the bitterness
    of disappointment?
Shall not the hate of men, and vengeance, fiercely
    pursuing,

Hunt down the wretched being that sinneth in his grave?
He fancied his idol self safe from the wrath of his fellows,
But Hades rose as he came in, to point at him the finger
    of scorn;
And again must he meet that orphan-maid to answer her
    face to face,
And her wrongs shall cling around his neck, to hinder him
    from rising with the just:
For his last most solemn act hath linked his name with
    liar,
And the crime of Ananias is branded on his brow!

IBID.

The Art of Giving (1850)

YET heed thou wisely this; give seldom to thy better;
For such obtrusive boon shall savour of presumption;
Or, if his courteous bearing greet thy proffered kindness,
Shall not thine independent honesty be vexed at the
    semblance of a bribe?
Moreover, heed thou this; give to thine equal charily,
The occasion fair and fitting, the gift well chosen and
    desired:
Hath he been prosperous and blest? a flower may show
    thy gladness;
Is he in need? with liberal love, tender him the well-filled
    purse:
Disease shall welcome friendly care in grapes and precious
    unguents;
And when a darling child hath died, give praise, and
    hope, and sympathy.
Yet once more, heed thou this; give to the poor discreetly,
Nor suffer idle sloth to lean upon thy charitable arm:
To diligence give, as to an equal, on just and fit occasion;
Or he bartereth his hard-earned self-reliance for the
    casual lottery of gifts.

The timely loan hath added nerve, where easy liberality
   would palsy;
Work and wages make a light heart, but the mendicant
   asketh with a heavy spirit.

IBID., 2ND SERIES.

JOHN CLOSE (1816–91)

JOHN CLOSE ("Poet Close"), a printer at Kirkby Stephen, astonished the thoughtful by suddenly appearing in the Civil List of 1860 with a pension of fifty pounds, by favour of Palmerston. Questions were asked in the House of Commons. It appeared that the poet, whose reputation had not until then spread beyond the boundaries of Westmorland, had for some years been indefatigably bombarding the nobility and gentry of the neighbourhood with rhyme, and that his supporters included Lord Lonsdale and Lord Carlisle; both, like Godolphin, good judges of a horse. Mr. Close's pension was at once cancelled in favour of a grant of one hundred pounds from the Royal Bounty, and from this time to his death he added to his income by thrusting his compositions on visitors (already numbed and dazed by the Wordsworth atmosphere) to the Lakes. W. S. Gilbert toyed with him in *Ferdinando and Elvira, or the Gentle Pieman.*

Mr. Close's reflections on steam may be compared with T. Baker's; but his theology is more decisive.

The Beelah Viaduct

O WONDROUS age! a wondrous age we live in,
  When Stainmore echoes with the awful din;
What novel sounds the eighty men are giving,
  While fixing firm the iron pillars in. . . .

All hail to Steam! all hail to men of Brain,
  Who sweep all obstacles before them,
Cut down the hills, and through the mountains bore,
  And make admiring crowds adore them. . . .

"The cloud-cap't Towers, the solemn Temples,"
  (As Shakespeare tells us in his verse sublime)
Our Bridge at last shall crumble—pass away—
  When there shall also be an end of Time.

Nay, "the great Globe itself," he plainly says,
   Shall disappear, and then be seen no more;
We don't believe this creed—our world will still
   Move round the sun as she hath done before.

But when "The Archangel's trump shall sound"
   (As good John Wesley piously sings),
May we among the heavenly host be found,
   When we have bid farewell to earthly things.

Haloes, Not Hats

AROUND the gods, each seated on a throne,
   The poets, crown'd like royal kings they sat.
Around their heads a dazzling halo shone,
   No need of mortal robes, or any hat.
Their curly locks, as white as driven snow,
   Hung down like shining frosted silver threads;
And oh! their eyes, so full of joy they beam'd
   And sparkled in their grand majestic heads.

                  A VISION OF THE GODS.

Mentem Mortalia Tangunt

AND have we lost another friend?
   How sad the news to tell!
Alas! poor Mr. Yarker's gone—
   Hark to the tolling bell!
Alas! how many now drop off—
   What numbers are unwell;
Another mortal borne away—
   Hark to the tolling bell!

      IN RESPECTFUL MEMORY OF MR. YARKER.

SYDNEY THOMPSON DOBELL (1824-74)

DOBELL's collaboration in 1854 with Alexander Smith in a volume of sonnets on the Crimean War moved the critic of *Blackwood's* to describe him and his partner as founders of the Spasmodic School. He wrote a fair amount of verse alone: it is all manly and vigorous, sometimes more. He was a hospitable, cultivated, and charming man, a friend of Tennyson, Carlyle, and Rossetti, and fully shared that contemporary enthusiasm for Mazzini's and Garibaldi's Italy which spoiled the earthly Paradise for so many.

Whether Dobell's Muse exhibits spasms in the ensuing dramatic fragment is a matter for discussion. Certainly the Monk's remarks to the revellers are slightly more than subacid; but it might with justice be urged that the old Italian custom of waltzing on mothers' graves required a sharp reprimand.

A Timely Hint

SCENE: *A plain in Italy.*   TIME: *Evening*

Youths and Maidens, singing as they waltz.

SING lowly, foot slowly, oh, why should we chase
The hour that gives heav'n to this earthly embrace?
To-morrow, to-morrow, is dreary and lonely;
Then love as they love, who would live to love only!
Closer yet, eyes of jet—breasts fair and sweet—
No eyes flash like those eyes that flash as they meet!
Weave brightly, wear lightly, the warm-woven chain,
Love on for to-night if we ne'er love again.
Fond youths! happy maidens! we are not alone!
Bright steps and sweet voices keep pace with our own;

Love-lorn Lusignuolo, the soft-sighing breeze,
The rose with the zephyr, the wind with the trees—
While heav'n, blushing pleasure, is full of love-notes,
Soft down the sweet measure the fairy world floats.

*The Monk advances, meets the dancers, and points to the turf
    at their feet.*

The Monk. Do you see nothing there—
There, where the unrespective grass grows green—
There, at your very feet?   Nay, not one step!
'Twould touch it! 'twould profane it!   Palsied be
The limb that treads that ground!   There is a grave—
There is a grave; I saw it with these eyes!
I saw it—saw it with these eyes; it holds—
It holds—oh, Heaven!—my mother.
One of the Revellers.   Peace, good Padre,
Look to thy beads.   The turf is level here.
Comrades! strike up!—"Sing lowly, foot——"
The Monk.   Who steps,
Steps first on me!   I say there is a grave—
I say it is my mother's;—that I loved her,
Ay, loved her, with more passion than the maddest
Lover among you clasps his one-day wife!
And I steal forth to keep my twilight vigil,
And you come here to dance upon my heart.
You come, and with the world at will, for dalliance—
The whole hot world—deny me that small grave,
Whose bitter margin these poor knees know better
Than your accustom'd feet the well-worn path
To your best harlot's bow'r.   The turf is fair!
Have I not kept it green with tears, my mother?
You lustful sons of lax-eyed lewdness, do you
Come here to sing above her bones and mock me
Because my flesh and blood cry out God save them?

                                        THE ROMAN.

EDWARD ROBERT BULWER LYTTON, EARL OF LYTTON ("OWEN MEREDITH") (1831–91)

ALTHOUGH the poetical work of ROBERT LYTTON, first Earl of Lytton, British Ambassador in Paris from 1887 to 1891, never captured the contemporary taste like the richly gilt romances and plays of his more famous father Edward Bulwer-Lytton, Baron Lytton, it will be perceived from the extracts following that the Earl is fully capable of wielding his pen (as Scott said of Byron) with the easy negligence of a nobleman. His Lordship's models are to some extent Browning, Tennyson, Poe, and Wordsworth, and with these Alfred de Musset, under whose influence a British Muse indulges regrettably in much lemon-kid-gloved, tight-waisted, varnished-booted, patchouli-scented cynico - sentimentalism connected with Marquises, lights-o'-love, and the odalisques and indiscretions of the *beau monde*: for example, such ladies as Clarisse, who

> "with a smile has subsided, opprest—
> Half, perhaps, by Champagne . . . half, perhaps, by affection"—

into the arms of a taciturn *milord anglais*, on what is probably a pale lilac-brocaded ottoman.

Observe the succinct and sufficient explanation of the Italian lady's ceasing to sing, and admire the smooth flow of rhythm in the financial item. It might be gathered at a careless glance that "Irene" in the second stanza of our third extract is an iambus, "I-reen," in the Overseas style. Study of the metre will show that this is not so.

Check to Song

I DREAM'D that I walk'd in Italy,
　　When the day was going down,
By a water that silently wander'd by
　　Thro' an old dim-lighted town,

Till I came to a palace fair to see.
　　Wide open the windows were
My love at a window sat; and she
　　Beckon'd me up the stair. . . .

When I came to the little rose-colour'd room,
　　From the curtains out flew a bat.
The window was open: and in the gloom
　　My love at the window sat.

She sat with her guitar on her knee,
　　But she was not singing a note,
For someone had drawn (ah, who could it be?)
　　A knife across her throat.

GOING BACK AGAIN.

Financial Note

A FORTNIGHT ago a report about town
Made me most apprehensive.　Alas and alas!
I at once wrote and warn'd you.　Well, now let that pass.
A run on the Bank about five days ago
Confirm'd my forebodings too terribly, though.
I drove down to the City at once: found the door
Of the Bank closed: the Bank had stopp'd payment
　　at four.
Warrant out for MacNab; but MacNab was abroad:
Gone—we cannot tell where.　I endeavour'd to get
Information: have learn'd nothing certain as yet—
Not even the way that old Ridley was gone:
Or with those securities what he had done:
Or whether they had been already call'd out:
If they are not, their fate is, I fear, past a doubt.

LUCILE.

The Count and the Lady

THERE was nothing but darkness, and midnight,
   And tempest, and storm, in the breast
Of the Count Rinaldo Rinaldi,
   As his foot o'er the black marble prest:—
The glimmering black marble stair
   Where the weed in the green ooze is clinging,
That leads to the garden so fair
   Where the nightingales softly are singing,—
   Where the minstrels new music are stringing,
And the dancers for dancing prepare.

There rustles a robe of white satin:
   There's a footstep falls light by the stair:
There rustles a robe of white satin:
   There's a gleaming of soft golden hair:
And the Lady Irene Ricasoli
   Stands near the cypress tree there,—
   Near Mnemosyne's statue so fair,—
The Lady Irene Ricasoli,
   With the light in her long golden hair. . . .

"None heeds us, belovèd Irene!
   None will mark if we linger or fly.
Amid the mad masks in yon revel,
   There is not an ear or an eye,—
Not one,—that will gaze or will listen;
   And save the small star in the sky
Which, to light us, so softly doth glisten,
   There is none to pursue us, Irene.
   O love me, O save me, I die!
I am thine, O be mine, O belovèd!

"Fly with me, Irene, Irene!
   The moon drops: the morning is near,

R

My gondola waits by the garden,
    And fleet is my own gondolier!"

What the Lady Irene Ricasoli
    By Mnemosyne's statue in stone,
Where she leaned, 'neath the black cypress tree,
    To the Count Rinaldo Rinaldi
    Replied then, it never was known,
And known, now, it never will be.

But the moon hath been melted in morning:
    And the lamps in the windows are dead:
And the gay cavaliers from the terrace,
    And the ladies they laugh'd with, are fled;
And the music is husht in the viols:
    And the minstrels, and dancers, are gone;
And the nightingales now in the garden
    From singing have ceased, one by one:
But the Count Rinaldo Rinaldi
    Still stands, where he last stood, alone,
'Neath the black cypress tree, near the water,
    By Mnemosyne's statue in stone.

O'er his spirit was silence and midnight,
    In his breast was the calm of despair.
He took, with a smile, from a casket
    A single soft curl of gold hair,—
    A wavy warm curl of gold hair,
And into the black-bosom'd water
    He flung it athwart the black stair.

                    COUNT RINALDO RINALDI.

Sordid Scene

                                    PALE
Thro' the thick vagueness of the vaporous night,
From the dark alley, with a clouded light,
Two rheumy, melancholy lampions flare.

They are the eyes of the Police.

                             In there,
Down the dark archway, thro' the greasy door,
Passionately pushing past the three or four
Complacent constables that cluster'd round
A costermonger, in gutter found
Incapably, but combatively, drunk,
The woman hurried. Thro' the doorway slunk
A peaky pinch'd-up child with frighten'd face.
Important witness in some murder case
About to come before the magistrate
To-morrow.

                                  Misery.

GEORGE EVELEIGH (*fl.* 1863)

In October 1863 *The Reader*, a serious if short-lived London review, published a notice of a work in the heroic metre by G. Eveleigh, M.R.C.S., etc., entitled *Science Revealed; a Poem, descriptive of the Works of Creation and the Truth of Scripture Record.* In his preface the poet declares his intention of reconciling some of the supposed differences between Scripture and Science, and of proving "the words of Scripture to be verbatimly correct and elegantly concise." He adds: "I have chosen poetic composition . . . as that by which scope and force are most readily attained and perpetuated." The reviewer of *The Reader* thought this rather odd, but the verse still odder.

Mr. Eveleigh's best work is contained in the passage following, which hardly needs annotation. If man (argues the poet, leading up to it) is to deal in mercy like his Maker, he must be a company promoter. The rhythmic surge of the blank verse, its rich yet sober texture, the sonorous clang of such a line as:

"To each a dividend—say, six per cent,"

are all admirable, though one cannot but believe that a more technical word than "prey" in the fourth line might have suggested itself to the poet on further consideration.

A Divine Mission

If, then, the State will but assistance lend
To give security to Companies,
The Public Companies with monied wings
Will fly like eagles to the scent of prey,
And every nook and corner of the world
Will find its Companies of men at work;
And, for the aid each Company receives,

Each Company could well afford to pay,
Out of its surplus revenues, the State;
If out of three but two a surplus have,
Two-thirds of each will reimburse the State,
And hold one-third a bonus to account,
Which gives the State two-thirds for profit too,
And two to reimburse the one that's lost.
Thus, if a Government agrees to give,
Whenever Public Companies are formed,
To each a dividend—say, six per cent
Per annum for a certain fixèd time,
And for security inspects accounts—
Then, of the profits which each yieldeth more
Than the same dividend of six per cent,
Two-thirds the Government itself shall claim,
The other third remaining to afford
The Company an extra dividend.

SCIENCE REVEALED.

EDWARD EDWIN FOOT (*fl.* 1867)

MR. FOOT, of Her Majesty's Customs, has a claim possibly on lovers of verse but certainly on lovers of the footnote, which may have been named after him. No English poet before or since has ever taken such pains to make his meaning clear and to guarantee the authenticity of his statements. As one example out of a hundred we may take his poem on the Lovers' Leap, the beauty-spot on the Dart, which the Prince Consort visited in 1852. The Prince, sings the poet:

> turned around anew,
> And bade the lovely spot adieu,
> Expressing pleasure at the glorious scene."

To which he adds in a footnote: "This is stated on the authority of Mr. G. Sparkes, of Ashburton, who had the honour of conducting His Royal Highness and suite through this part of the journey."

Mr. Foot's one volume came out in 1867, on the recommendation of Sir F. H. Doyle, Bart., Receiver-General of H.M. Customs. The footnotes appended to the extracts following are his own.

Disaster at Sea

> THE captain scans the ruffled zone,[1]
> And heeds the wind's increasing scope;
> He knows full well, and reckons on
> His seamanship, but God's his hope. . . .

[1] A figurative expression, intended by the Author to signify the horizon.

Look, look ye down the plumbless deep,
  See,[1] if ye can, their lifeless forms!—
Here laid, poor things! across a steep,
  An infant in its mother's arms;

There, it may be, a man and wife,
  (Embracing either now as when
They went to rest, at night, in life),
  Are resting in a turbid glen.

THE HOMEWARD-BOUND PASSENGER SHIP.

A State Occasion

ONE circle round our Sun—and o'er—[2]
Is perfected, since forth there stray'd [3]
In youth a fair Princess,
From whom fell liquid drops of love—
Love-crystals of her wedding tour.
Though griev'd, the fair-form'd gentle maid
(Whom God was pleas'd to bless)
With modest courage sweetly strove
And conquer'd it!—Joy helping her.

Those moments sad, Time soon spent out:
Her EDWARD, yet afar,
Beheld her with bright vision's eye.
She wiped away the pearly tear,
And tripp'd on deck.   Then 'rose a shout
For Denmark's shooting star—
Resounding thro' the azure sky!
  Silently sped the ship over the sea:
  EDWARD beheld his Bride, happy and free.

CHRISTENING THE PRINCE.

[1] Imagine.
[2] The reader will please to observe that lines 1st and 5th,
2nd and 6th, 3rd and 7th, etc., have rhythmical terminations.
[3] The Author seeks indulgence in using the word "stray'd."

The Good Young Squire

It hap'd a gentle youth—a lordly heir
To vast domains—did annually repair
Unto this country mansion, to renew
His pleasant visits to his Uncle Prew:
The fair-hair'd stripling proved a welcome guest,
For there was something in his generous breast
Which won for him the universal mark
(From Bishop Butler,[1] to the parish-clerk),
Of friendship—nay, the love of one and all;
The village matrons, all were wont to call
Him "the young Squire"; and as he pass'd their way
They'd call their daughters from the washing-tray,
Or spinning-wheel, or the old-fashion'd loom,
Or in the midst of scrubbing out a room,
Or at the pigs' sty—where they were intent
Upon the beast,[2] which paid the yearly rent;
And forth they'd come.

        Jane Hollybrand; or, Virtue Rewarded.

A Graceful Divine

The following day, about th' eleventh hour,
Jane heard a "tap-tap" at the parlour door,
So, suddenly uprising on her feet,
Prepared herself the visitor to meet,—
"The Reverend Alexander Gordon Jay," [3]
(Most popular grammar-master of the day,
Within a circle of near thirty miles—
A man belov'd by most fair juveniles;

[1] The (imaginary) bishop of the diocese.
[2] The value of ——.
[3] D.D.

Of stature small, but of capacious tact;
And of his person wondrously exact.)—
Who with obeisance and with dexter hand
Proffer'd his friendship to Jane Hollybrand;
Jane fain reciprocated his intent
And lent herself to the first rudiment;

Thus so far pleased with all that he desired,
The doctor bowed, and gracefully retired.

IBID.

A Lisp in Numbers

ALTHO' we [1] mourn for one now gone,
And he—that grey-hair'd Palmerston,[2]
　　We will give God the praise,—
For he, beyond the age of man,[3]
Eleven years had over-ran
　　Within two equal days.

[1] The nation.
[2] The Right Honourable Henry John Temple, Viscount Palmerston, K.G., G.C.B., etc. (the then Premier of the British Government), died at "Brockett Hall," Herts., at a quarter to eleven o'clock in the forenoon of Wednesday, 18th October, 1865, aged eighty-one years (all but two days), having been born on the 20th October, 1784. The above lines were written on the occasion of his death.
[3] Scriptural limitation.

ADAM LINDSAY GORDON (1833–70)

Adam Lindsay Gordon went from Oxford to Australia in 1853 and joined the mounted police as a trooper. In 1865 he sat as Member for Victoria in the House of Assembly, in 1867 he left politics and opened a livery-stable at Ballarat. In the same year he published his first volume of poems, *Sea Spray and Smoke Drift*. In 1870 he published *Bush Ballads*, and later in the year committed suicide.

The vigorous, open-air quality of his verse is amply shown in the extracts following, and the call sounded in *Ye Wearie Wayfarer* once more reminds Imperial thinkers that the future of Empire depends on Tattersall's.

From "*Ashtaroth*," a Drama

[*Hugo's astronomical studies are interrupted by a summons to supper.*]

WHAT share have I at their festive board?
  Their mirth I can only mar;
To me no pleasure their cups afford,
  Their songs on my silence jar.
With an aching heart and a throbbing brain,
  And yet with a hopeful heart,
I must toil and strain with the planets again
  When the rays of the sun depart;
He who must needs with the topers tope
  And the feasters feast in the hall,
How can he hope with a matter to cope
  That is immaterial?

230

[*Harold has just gone out.*]

    Thora. Husband, that man is ill and weak;
      On foot he goes and alone
   Through a barren moor in a night-storm bleak.
   Eric. Now I wonder where he has gone!
   Hugo. Indeed, I have not the least idea;
      The man is certainly mad.
   He wedded my sister Dorothea,
      And used her cruelly bad.

[*Eric resolves to visit his mother.*]

   Hugo. The morn is fair, the weary miles
   Will shorten 'neath the summer's wiles,
   Pomona in the orchard smiles,
      And in the meadow, Flora.
   And I have roused a chosen band
   For escort through the troubled land:
   And shaken Elspeth by the hand,
      And said farewell to Thora. . . .
   Now, Eric, change thy plans and ride
   With us, thou hast no ties, no bride.
   Eric. Nay, ties I have, and time and tide,
      Thou knowest, wait for no man;
   And I go north; God's blessing shuns
   The dwellings of forgetful sons,
   That proverb he may read who runs,
      In Christian lore or Roman.

   My good old mother, she hath heard,
   For twelve long months, from me no word;
   At thought of her my heart is stirr'd
      And even mine eyes grow moister.
   Greet Ursula from me; her fame
   Is known to all. A nobler dame,
   Since days of Clovis, ne'er became
      The inmate of a cloister.

Our paths diverge, yet we may go
Together for a league or so;
I, too, will join thy band below
    When thou thy bugle windest.   [*Eric goes out.*
Hugo. From weaknesses we stand afar,
    On us unpleasantly they jar;
    And yet the stoutest-hearted are
        The gentlest and the kindest.
My mother loved me tenderly;
Alas! her only son was I.
I shudder'd, but my lids were dry,
    By death made orphan newly.
A braver man than me, I swear,
Who never comprehended fear,
Scarce names his mother, and the tear,
    Unbidden, starts unduly.

The Fight in the Cave

FLASH! flash! bang! bang! and we blazed away,
    And the grey roof reddened and rang;
Flash! flash! and I felt his bullet flay
    The tip of my ear.   Flash! bang!
Bang! flash! and my pistol arm fell broke;
    I struck with my left hand then—
Struck at a corpse through a cloud of smoke—
    I had shot him dead in his den!

WOLF AND HOUND.

A Warning

IF once we efface the joys of the chase
    From the land, and outroot the Stud,
GOOD-BYE TO THE ANGLO-SAXON RACE!
    FAREWELL TO THE NORMAN BLOOD!

YE WEARIE WAYFARER.

JULIA MOORE (1847–1920)

THE death ten years ago, at an advanced age, of JULIA MOORE, the Sweet Singer of Michigan, passed almost unnoticed in the American Press, which had welcomed her poems in 1876 with such jubilation. Mrs. Moore, a farmer's wife, lived all her life among those spacious rolling pastures (where men are Men) of which a later native poet has well sung:

> "That's why I wish again
> That I was in Michigan,
> Down on the farm."

Her first volume, *The Sweet Singer of Michigan Salutes the Public*, afterwards known as *The Sentimental Song Book*, was rapturously received, especially by Bill Nye and by Mark Twain, who admitted much later that it had given him joy for twenty years; and the appreciations of these and fifty other critics, which the poet accepted as genuine, did much to make her book a best-seller and send it into three editions. By 1878, when *A Few Choice Words to the Public, with New and Original Poems, by Julia A. Moore* appeared, her vogue had waned, and she published no more verse. In her preface to this volume she says of its predecessor: "Although some of the newspapers speak against it, its sale has steadily progressed. Thanks to the Editors that has spoken in favor of my writings; may they ever be successful. The Editors that has spoken in a scandalous manner, have went beyond reason. . . ." And she adds, defending herself against these evil men, that "Literary is a work very difficult to do," and that poetry from the heart has more power than poetry from the head. "If all books could be read as I am sure you love to read this one," she says elsewhere, "there might be less ignorance and crime in the world, and I would be well paid for the valuable time I have spent in doing good to mankind." A recent editor, Mr. Walter Blair of the University of Chicago, justly observes that it is high time for Posterity to pay its debt to Julia Moore.

The Sweet Singer's verse is concerned to a large extent with total abstinence and violent death—the great Chicago fire, the railway disaster of Ashtabula, the Civil War, the yellow fever epidemic in the South. She sings death by drowning, by smallpox, by fits, accidents by lightning-stroke and sleigh. "Julia is worse than a Gatling gun," wrote Bill Nye; "I have counted twenty-one killed and nine wounded, in the small volume she has given to the public." She also greatly relishes normal infant mortality, especially in cases where the little victim possesses blue eyes and curling golden hair; but in her celebrations of the centenary of American independence she strikes the sterner Kipling note more than once. Observe that our first specimen is a tonic antidote to the dithyrambs of T. Baker and Poet Close, and that the study of Byron is illuminated by the generous sympathy (Byron's bad character notwithstanding) of one misjudged poet for another.

Steam : *The Seamy Side*

[*Air : "Gently Down the Stream of Time"*]

HAVE you heard of the dreadful fate
　　Of Mr. P. P. Bliss and wife?
Of their death I will relate,
　　And also others lost their life;
Ashtabula Bridge disaster,
　　Where so many people died
Without a thought that destruction
　　Would plunge them 'neath the wheel of tide.

Chorus

Swiftly passed the engine's call,
　　Hastening souls on to death,
Warning not one of them all;
　　It brought despair right and left.

Among the ruins are many friends,
　　Crushed to death amidst the roar,
On one thread all may depend,
　　And hope they've reached the other shore.

P. P. Bliss showed great devotion
    To his faithful wife, his pride,
When he saw that she must perish
    He died a martyr by her side.

P. P. Bliss went home above—
    Left all friends, earth, and fame,
To rest in God's holy love;
    Left on earth his work and name.
The people love his work by numbers,
    It is read by great and small,
He by it will be remembered,
    He has left it for us all.

His good name from time to time
    Will rise on land and sea;
It is known in distant climes,
    Let it echo wide and free.
One good man among the number,
    Found sweet rest in a short time,
His weary soul may sweetly slumber
    Within the vale, heaven sublime.

THE ASHTABULA DISASTER.

Byron : a Critical Survey

"LORD BYRON" was an Englishman
    A poet I believe,
His first works in old England
    Was poorly received.
Perhaps it was "Lord Byron's" fault
    And perhaps it was not.
His life was full of misfortunes,
    Ah, strange was his lot.

The character of "Lord Byron"
    Was of a low degree,
Caused by his reckless conduct,
    And bad company.
He sprung from an ancient house,
    Noble, but poor, indeed.
His career on earth, was marred
    By his own misdeeds.

Generous and tender-hearted,
    Affectionate by extreme,
In temper he was wayward,
    A poor "Lord" without means;
Ah, he was a handsome fellow
    With great poetic skill,
His great intellectual powers
    He could use at his will.

He was a sad child of nature,
    Of fortune and of fame;
Also sad child to society,
    For nothing did he gain
But slander and ridicule,
    Throughout his native land.
Thus the "poet of the passions,"
    Lived, unappreciated, man.

Yet at the age of 24
    "Lord Byron" then had gained
The highest, highest pinnacle
    Of literary fame.
Ah, he had such violent passions
    They was beyond his control,
Yet the public with its justice
    Sometimes would him extol.

Sometimes again "Lord Byron"
  Was censured by the press,
Such obloquy, he could not endure,
  So he done what was the best.
He left his native country,
  This great unhappy man;
The only wish he had, "'tis said,"
  He might die, sword in hand.

He had joined the Grecian Army,
  This man of delicate frame;
And there he died in a distant land,
  And left on earth his fame.
"Lord Byron's" age was 36 years,
  Then closed the sad career,
Of the most celebrated "Englishman"
  Of the nineteenth century.

LORD BYRON'S LIFE.

A Noble Structure

IN the year eighteen seventy-six,
  A Fourth of July celebration
Was held in Grand Rapids city
  In honor to our nation.
The largest city in the county of Kent,
  Is this city, and it is respected,
For thousands of people was here to see
  The beautiful arch erected.

The paintings and mottoes on the arch
  Was viewed by many people;
It was Colonel Joseph Penney's design,
  And his work could not be equalled.
Mr. C. H. Gifford was architect,
  He formed the noble structure,
A memento to the Centennial year,
  A pride of our nation's culture.

A cabin was built, too, I believe,
  That nicely represented
One that the traders built years ago,
  This was the only one invented.
Ten thousand people respected it,
  This token of early years, with joy;
The honor of this little hut
  Was due to Mr. Godfroy.

THE CENTENNIAL CELEBRATION.

Hic Finis Rapto

I

FOR he was sick, and very bad—
  Poor boy, he thought, no doubt,
If he came home in a smoking car
  His money would hold out.
He started to come back alone—
  He came one-third the way—
One evening in the car alone
  His spirit fled away.

JOHN ROBINSON.

II

Minnie May House she had to go,
  And leave her friends that loved her so—
She was a girl in her teens,
  As lovely a flower as e'er was seen.

WILLIAM HOUSE AND FAMILY.

III

God has took their little treasure,
  And his name I'll tell you now,
He has gone from earth forever,
  Their little Charles Henry House.

LITTLE HENRY.

IV

Carrie's age was twenty-three,
  A married lady, too, was she·—
A mournful parting had to be,
  From Carrie Monro.

It's just before her spirit fled
  Her husband stood by her bed;
"Prove faithful, birdie, to me," said
  Sweet Carrie Monro.

CARRIE MONRO.

V

"She was buried on her wedding-day," these words a
    friend gave,
Her lover went as a mourner, a mourner to her grave,
His name was Forest Dilly, a young man over west,
He loved this handsome Maryette, the lily of the west.

MARYETTE MYERS.

VI

While eating dinner, this dear little child
  Was choked on a piece of beef.
Doctors came, tried their skill awhile,
  But none could give relief. . . .
Her friends and schoolmates will not forget
  Little Libbie that is no more;
She is waiting on the shining step,
  To welcome home friends once more.

LITTLE LIBBIE.

The Poet is Scornful

PERHAPS you've read the papers,
    Containing my interview;
I hope you kind good people
    Will not believe it true.
Some Editors of the papers
    They thought it would be wise
To write a column about me
    So they filled it up with lies.

The papers have ridiculed me
    A year and a half or more,
Such slander as the interview
    I never read before.
Some reporters and editors
    Are versed in telling lies.
Others it seems are willing
    To let industry rise.

              TO MY FRIENDS AND CRITICS.

A Call (1876)

IT is now one hundred years
    Or just one century,
Stood grand this good old nation,
    And our forefathers fought
That we may not be a slave—
    A slave to the monarchy of England.

Revolutionary war was fought
    With the British, this we hear,
To make this an independent nation;
    We, the independent men,
We will not be a slave,
    To bond-holders in our nation.

              HURRAH FOR COOPER AND CARY

Anti-Bacchics

I

MANY a man joined the club
  That never drank a drachm,
These noble men were kind and brave
  They care not for the slang—
The slang they meet on every side:
  "You're a reform drunkard, too;
You've joined the Red Ribbon brigade,
  Among the drunkard crew."

TEMPERANCE REFORM CLUBS.

II

Ah, from this Temperance army,
  Your feet shall never stray,
Your mind will then be balmy
  If you keep the shining way.

THE TEMPERANCE ARMY.

ALFRED, LORD TENNYSON (1809–92)

THE nobly sonorous Muse of LORD TENNYSON, when called on officially to celebrate such a public event as the International Exhibition, the opening of a new railway, or the illness of an aunt by marriage, once removed, of the R—y—l F—m—ly, uttered no complaint but stoically tucked up her sleeves of white samite and got on with the job; for if she was a perfect lady (one remembers the profound reply of the book-loving London policeman to Mr. Arthur Symons when asked if he ever read Tennyson: "No, sir. . . . Isn't he rather a ladylike writer?") she was also British to the bone, and her devotion to duty deserves nothing but praise.

She occasionally gave expression, of her own accord, to another deep-rooted British trait. She could be a terrible snob. Her ecstasies over the Lord of Burleigh's condescension to the village maid awake echoes of Putney rather than Parnassus, and breathing in quick rapturous gasps she brings her lyric doggerel to an end none too soon. She was not quite at her ease with another member of the lower classes, Enoch Arden, and of her refined hint at the nature of his trade Walter Bagehot drily remarked, "So much has not often been made of selling fish." Compare Crabbe's blunter handling of the *motif*:

> "To town came quiet Peter with his fish,
> And had of all a civil word and wish."

Compare, also, Iphigenia's fate with the similar fate of the unfortunate Italian lady in Lytton's verse, already quoted. "What touching simplicity," observed Lockhart, "what pathetic resignation—he cut her throat; nothing more."

Ode

Sung at the Opening of the International Exhibition

I

UPLIFT a thousand voices full and sweet
   In this wide hall with earth's invention stored,

Mr. Tennyson, reading "In Memoriam" to his Sovereign

And praise the invisible universal Lord,
Who lets once more in peace the nations meet,
  Where Science, Art, and Labour have outpour'd
Their myriad horns of plenty at our feet.

II

O silent father of our Kings to be,
Mourn'd in this golden hour of jubilee,
For this, for all, we weep our thanks to thee.

III

The world-compelling plan was thine,—
And lo! the long laborious miles
Of Palace; lo! the giant aisles,
Rich in model and design;
Harvest-tool and husbandry,
Loom and wheel and enginery,
Secrets of the sullen mine,
Steel and gold, and corn and wine,
Fabric rough, or fairy-fine,
Sunny tokens of the Line,
Polar marvels, and a feast
Of wonder, out of West and East,
And shapes and hues of Art divine!
All of beauty, all of use,
That one fair planet can produce,
  Brought from under every star,
Blown from over every main,
And mixt, as life is mixt with pain,
  The works of peace with works of war.

IV

Is the goal so far away?
Far, how far no tongue can say,
Let us dream our dream to-day.

V

O ye, the wise who think, the wise who reign,
From growing commerce loose her latest chain,
And let the fair white-wing'd peacemaker fly
To happy havens under all the sky,
And mix the seasons and the golden hours;
Till each man find his own in all men's good,
And all men work in noble brotherhood,
Breaking their mailed fleets and armed towers,
And ruling by obeying Nature's powers,
And gathering all the fruits of earth and crown'd with
　　all her flowers.

The Lord of Burleigh

In her ear he whispers gaily,
　　"If my heart by signs can tell,
Maiden, I have watch'd thee daily,
　　And I think thou lov'st me well."
She replies, in accents fainter,
　　"There is none I love like thee."
He is but a landscape-painter,
　　And a village maiden she.
He to lips, that fondly falter,
　　Presses his without reproof:
Leads her to the village altar,
　　And they leave her father's roof.
"I can make no marriage present:
　　Little can I give my wife.
Love will make our cottage pleasant,
　　And I love thee more than life."
They by parks and lodges going
　　See the lordly castles stand:
Summer woods, about them blowing,
　　Made a murmur in the land.

From deep thought himself he rouses,
  Says to her that loves him well,
"Let us see these handsome houses
  Where the wealthy nobles dwell."
So she goes by him attended,
  Hears him lovingly converse,
Sees whatever fair and splendid
  Lay betwixt his home and hers.
Parks with oak and chestnut shady,
  Parks and order'd gardens great,
Ancient homes of lord and lady,
  Built for pleasure and for state.
All he shows her makes him dearer:
  Evermore she seems to gaze
On that cottage growing nearer,
  Where they twain will spend their days.
O but she will love him truly!
  He shall have a cheerful home;
She will order all things duly,
  When beneath his roof they come.
Thus her heart rejoices greatly,
  Till a gateway she discerns
With armorial bearings stately,
  And beneath the gate she turns;
Sees a mansion more majestic
  Than all those she saw before:
Many a gallant gay domestic
  Bows before him at the door.
And they speak in gentle murmur,
  When they answer to his call,
While he treads with footstep firmer,
  Leading on from hall to hall.
And while now she wonders blindly,
  Nor the meaning can divine,
Proudly turns he round and kindly,
  "All of this is mine and thine."
Here he lives in state and bounty,

Lord of Burleigh, fair and free,
Not a lord in all the county
  Is so great a lord as he.
All at once the colour flushes
  Her sweet face from brow to chin:
As it were with shame she blushes,
  And her spirit changed within.
Then her countenance all over
  Pale again as death did prove:
But he clasp'd her like a lover,
  And he cheer'd her soul with love.
So she strove against her weakness,
  Tho' at times her spirit sank:
Shaped her heart with woman's meekness
  To all duties of her rank:
And a gentle consort made he,
  And her gentle mind was such
That she grew a noble lady,
  And the people loved her much.
But a trouble weigh'd upon her,
  And perplex'd her, night and morn,
With the burthen of an honour
  Unto which she was not born.
Faint she grew, and ever fainter,
  And she murmur'd, "Oh, that he
Were once more that landscape-painter,
  Which did win my heart from me!"
So she droop'd and droop'd before him,
  Fading slowly from his side:
Three fair children first she bore him,
  Then before her time she died.
Weeping, weeping late and early,
  Walking up and pacing down,
Deeply mourn'd the Lord of Burleigh,
  Burleigh-house by Stamford-town.
And he came to look upon her,
  And he look'd at her and said,

"Bring the dress and put it on her,
   That she wore when she was wed."
Then her people, softly treading,
   Bore to earth her body, drest
In the dress that she was wed in,
   That her spirit might have rest.

Ocean-Spoil Alive, O!

So these were wed, and merrily rang the bells,
And merrily ran the years, seven happy years,
Seven happy years of health and competence,
And mutual love and honourable toil;
With children; first a daughter. In him woke,
With his first babe's first cry, the noble wish
To save all earnings to the uttermost,
And give his child a better bringing-up
Than his had been, or hers; a wish renew'd,
When two years after came a boy to be
The rosy idol of her solitudes,
While Enoch was abroad on wrathful seas,
Or often journeying landward; for in truth
Enoch's white horse, and Enoch's ocean-spoil
In ocean-smelling osier, and his face,
Rough-redden'd with a thousand winter gales,
Not only to the market-cross were known,
But in the leafy lanes behind the down,
Far as the portal-warding lion-whelp,
And peacock-yewtree of the lonely Hall,
Whose Friday fare was Enoch's ministering.

ENOCH ARDEN.

Riflemen Form

Be not deaf to the sound that warns,
Be not gull'd by a despot's plea!
Are figs of thistles? or grapes of thorns?
How can a despot feel with the Free?

Form, Form, Riflemen Form!
Ready, be ready to meet the storm!
Riflemen, Riflemen, Riflemen form!

Let your reforms for a moment go!
Look to your butts, and take good aims!
Better a rotten borough or so
Than a rotten fleet and a city in flames!
Storm, Storm, Riflemen form!
Ready, be ready against the storm!
Riflemen, Riflemen, Riflemen form!

PRINTED IN "THE TIMES," MAY 1859.

Iphigenia in Extremis

THE tall masts quiver'd as they lay afloat,
    The temples and the people and the shore;
One drew a sharp knife thro' my tender throat
    Slowly,—and nothing more.

A DREAM OF FAIR WOMEN
(ORIGINAL VERSION).

POSTPRANDIAL

The silent heavens have goings-on.
> Wordsworth, The Gipsies
> (Original Version).

The weed of a damsel when bound for her rest.
> Sir Walter Scott, The Bloody Vest.

This melancholy scene demands a groan.
> John Gay, Dione.

He wiped his iron eye and brow.
> Sir Walter Scott, The Lady of the Lake.

They went across the veldt
As hard as they could pelt.
> Alfred Austin on the Jameson Raid.

My drooping memory will not shun
The foaming grape of eastern France.
> Tennyson, In Memoriam.

How will sweet Ovid's ghost be pleas'd to hear
His fame augmented by a British peer!
> Dryden, To the Earl of Roscommon.

That is a work of waste and ruin;
Consider, Charles, what you are doing.
> Wordsworth.

The star-surveying sage close to his eye
Applies the sight-invigorating tube.

ROBERT BLAIR, THE GRAVE.

And now we have a boy—like me, they say,
Also I think a little bit like you.

GERALD GOULD.

At last, by favour of Almighty God,
With bellying sail the fathers made Cape Cod.

ALFRED AUSTIN, THE PILGRIM FATHERS.

'Tis eve in Heaven!   O! Let it be,
    It is so sweet to think that there,
When Earth moves onward bitterly,
    Repose is letting down her hair.

E. D. GIRDLESTONE, NOON.[1]

Ye monsters of the bubbling deep,
    Your Maker's praises shout,
Up from the sands, ye codlings, leap
    And wag your tails about.

A BOSTON HYMNODIST UNKNOWN.

But lo! with graceful motion there she swims,
    Gently removing each ambitious wave;
The crowding waves transported clasp her limbs;
    When, when, oh when, shall I such freedoms have?

ANON., TRANSLATION OF A LAPLAND LOVE-SONG.[2]

[1] Quoted in *The Oxford Ars Poetica*, 1853.
[2] *Spectator*, No. 406.

For me are homelier tasks prepared;
To the stone table in my garden
The Squire is come, and, as I guess,
His little ruddy daughter Bess
With Harry the Churchwarden.

WORDSWORTH, PROLOGUE TO PETER BELL
(ORIGINAL VERSION).

How shriek'd the hoarse ravens a knell!
    When vain and quite useless the rein,
All headlong together down fell
    The horse, the poor Lady, the Dean.
The Lady, by lace-braided hair
    Entangled in brambles was found,
Suspended unhurt in mid-air;
    The Dean met his death with the ground.

THE REV. SAMUEL BEWLEY,
THE RIVER DOVE: A LYRIC PASTORAL.

[THE END]

SUBJECT INDEX

ACT of Parliament, 13 Geo. III, c. 80, cited, 206

Adam, his internal fluids, 18

Alexandra, Queen, one of the Ancient Danes, 15; sheds liquid drops of love, 227; Denmark's shooting star, ibid.

Aliments, oily, their coy behaviour in the stomach, 61; tumults and horrors arising from their introduction, ibid.

Anatomist, impolite, receives a shock, 162

Angels, not immune from curiosity, 31, 162; give Mr. Purcell a flying lesson, 37; patrol the British sky, 47; invited to take up permanent quarters at Whitehall, 50; and Britons, mixed choir of, ibid.

Ankles, œdematous, S. Lee's, 146

Arden, Enoch, his expensive obsequies, 8; his early married life, 247

Astronomy, pursuit of, inconsistent with social obligations, 230

Author, Victorian, blessed with a mind, 209; his blooming fruits, 210

Azotic gas. *See* Nitrogen

Babylon, rightly served out, 101

Bacchanal, buried, 63

Bacon, a stubborn aliment, 61

Bagpipes, their silence regretted, 151

Baker, Mr., resources of the Muse strained by his recovery, 110; requests Miss Hoyland to own a mutual flame, ibid.

"Bang! flash!" παρὰ προσδοκίαν for "Flash! bang!" (q.v.), 232

Bards, dead, common objects of the sea-shore, 66

Bates, charming Mr., 49

Baths, cold, *see* Cistern, gelid; warm, recommended in moderation, 63

Beauties, well-baked, 5

Beaux, Irish, their grovelling minds, 194

Bedfordshire, departure for, imminent, 1

Beef, death-dealing, 239

Beethoven, light thrown on his ancestry, xv; his shaky octave-playing, 6

Beetle, flight of, described, 15; not addicted to vagabondage, 150; a child-lover, 171

Bilious attack, poetical description of a, 61

Bird. *See* Maiden, feathered

Bleaters, gouty, 76; how cured, 77. *See also* Sheep

Botanist, as mountaineer, inferior to goat, 82

Britain, her naval bloom, 73; shocks the Continent, 75; pessimistic forecast of her future, 137

Britons. *See under* Angels

Bryan, tragic bisection and deglutition of, 89

Bug, West Indian, life-history of, 90

Burials, mixed, 163

Burleigh, Lord, his involuntary erubescence, 33

Byron, Lord, believed to be a poet, 235; his low character, 236; his career sketched in a few bold strokes, 236–7

Cabbage, true-hearted, 22

Carrot, sluggish, 22

Charles II, his magnetic effect on the coast-line, 31; the Faculty get to work on, 32

Cheese, Cheshire, by whom digestible, 61

Christians, liable to leak, 4

Chyle, Adamic, 18; compared to Nile, 28; friendly, 61; nutrimental, 62

Cistern, gelid, fortifying effects of, 62

Clutterbuck and Co., their services requisitioned, 111

Company promoters, eighteenth-century, did not run to fat, 63; feather-beds appropriate to, ibid.

Constables, complacent, 223

Corpse, said to smile inaudibly, 2; flaccid, 3; incomparably attractive, 18

Costermonger, drunk and disorderly, 223

Cow, attention drawn to, by Tradition, 8

Creation, one vast Exchange, 72; staggers at atheist's nod, 174

Creator, the, given cause to blush by Mr. Merry, 119; admonished by Mr. Montgomery, 174

Critics, warned off by Mrs. Moore, 10; castigated by Mr. Tupper, 210

Crocodile, sincere tears of a, 41

Curses, various, xv, 33, 119, 218

Daughters of the plain, guileless, chased by Henry, 82; of the great, illustrious, recalled to their maternal duties, 95

David, King, blue-pencils a score of Mr. Purcell's, 37

Death. *See* Monster, grim

Dentist, refuge of the suffering fair, 13

Deprecation, yell of, emitted by scared native, 138

Dorsal region, bright, 1; lunar, glorious, 12

Drains. *See* Sewage system

Drunkards. *See* Bacchanal, Costermonger, *and* Feather-beds

Earl, a superb old, 177; rush of M.D.s to his deathbed, 178

Edward, inexplicable ignorance of, 149

Eggs, mention of, wrapped in elegant obscurity, 62

Elephant, not amphibious, 58

Eliza takes the children to see a battle, 106; gets it in the neck, ibid.

England, small but well known, 200; emphatically unde-generate, 202

Englishman, his heart a rich rough gem that leaps and strikes and glows and yearns, 200–1; sun never sets on his might, 201; thinks well of himself, ibid.

Ether, bales of, 41

False Gallia's sons. *See* Frenchmen

Feather, Cynthia's, weather forecasts based on, 23

Feather-beds, not to be grudged to company promoters and drunkards, 63; silk-worm's indifference to, 150

Feet, sore, how detected, 9

Female, scaly, not fettered by conventional morality, 59

Financier, death of an eminent, 195; Scottish, successful coup by a, 220

Fire, wetness not an attribute of, 28

Fish, Tennyson contrives to avoid mentioning, 247. *See also* Female, scaly

"Flash! bang!" subtly varied with "Bang! flash!" (q.v.), 232

Footmen, characteristic gaiety and gallantry of, 245

Free verse, Anna Matilda advocates, 122

Frenchmen, fraudful, mix sand with sugar, 90

Friendship, Mr. Frogley's complaint concerning, 12; female, lasting consolations of, 156

Frog, American, a simple-lifer, 19; Egyptian, sybaritic, 144

Gabriel, the Archangel, titivates himself, 25

Gases, goings-on of, 108

George II, his particularly nice virtues, 9; his half-share in the universe, 52; his fortunate philoprogenitiveness, 52, 54; his blooming honours, 68; his godlike appearance, ibid.

George III unlocks chaste Beauty's adamantine zone, 93; enters Paradise, 132

German place-names, the poet does his best with, 54

Gill, Harry, his extensive yet inadequate wardrobe, 144

Gloucester, Duke of, a heavy-weight, 31

Goats, Welsh, their agility envied by botanist, 82

Golf, a remedy for unemployment, 16

Gouge, Rev. T., brought to dust, 49

Grapes and embrocations, suitable gifts for invalids, 213

Grave, living, *see* Shark; rose-covered, 4, 160; suicide's, rendezvous at a, 86; mother's, habit of dancing on, reprobated, 218

Gravy, blood and, 16

Great Exhibition, the, its contents compendiously catalogued, 243

Guardian Angel, Miss Jewsbury's, has a pressing engagement, 151

Gunston, Mr., admits superiority of heavenly architecture, 48

Hags, midnight, damnèd vigils of, ignored by pensive poet, 137

Handkerchiefs, relays of, called for, 16

Harp-string, damped by poet's tears, 169

Hats, unfashionable in heaven, 216

Hatter affords relief to ram, 77

Heart wins over Art every time, 13

Heaven, system of bookkeeping in, 32; vogue of Mr. Purcell's music in, 37; unexpected grandeur of its architecture, 48; knowledge of languages useful in, ibid.; blasted, 188; haloes the only wear in, 216

Henry spares no expense in his nefarious designs on Jessy, 82
Henry II, urged to get a move on, 46; his pleasing anguish, ibid.
Hinds, salubrious, 14; athletic, 60. *See also* Swains
Hope, a high-kicker, 1
Hops need props, 97
Horns, Conchimarian, 185
Hottentots, uncommercial parricides, 77
Hull, lost property at, 150

Immortality, hope of, distinguishes man from silk-worm, 152
Incense of thanksgiving, upwafted from Leeds chimneys, 78
Inebriation, infantile, adjudged blameless, 96
Interview of Paolo with Francesca, 134; of Rev. Jay with Miss
Hollybrand, 228
Italy, not recommended to tourists, 125; examples of what
goes on there, 204, 219, 221
Ithuriel, the Archangel, shows Mr. Gunston round heaven, 48

Jay, Rev. Alexander Gordon, D.D., his capacious tact, 229
Jessy succumbs to Henry's wiles, 82; chased by birds and
lambs, 83; reproved by jasmines, ibid.; cut by neighbours,
ibid.; embarks for unspecified destination, 84; last seen
floating on watery plain, ibid.
Jewsbury, Miss, cheats time with stuffed owl, 151
Jonah takes his seat for a submarine jaunt, 65

Kilt, its degradation by youths' outfitters deprecated, 151
Kindred, Jonas, his deceptive stature, 3
Kleinhovia, a formidable nymph, 107

Lamprey, osculatory feats of, 108
Landscape-painter, typical courtship of village maiden by, 244
Lays, female, tuneful but immoral, 103
Lee, Miss R., said to resemble a cucumber, 184
Lee, Mrs. S., an aged woman, 146; her superior agility, ibid.
Lee, Simon, rumoured reduction of his stature, 145; conflicting
evidence concerning his age, ibid.; fore-and-aft view of his
coat, ibid.; his general appearance, and particularly his legs
and ankles, described, 146; location of his residence, ibid.;
stumped by a root, 147

Leeds, poetical aspects of, 78
Lewdness, lax-eyed, lustful sons of, 218
Liverpool, rapture experienced at, 196

Maiden, feathered, uncontrolled appetites of, 59; Swiss, coming-on disposition of, 190
Mansion, heavenly, kept vacant for the Warner family, 49; country, superlatively majestic, 245
Manure, adjudged a fit subject for the Muse, 91
Mead, awful Mr., 49
Mechanic, pale, exhibited in a hurry to wallow in vice, 137
Milk, periphrastically indicated, 62, 95
Mind, balmy, how to preserve a, 241
Mole, not addicted to lacustrine explorations, 58; has its mission in life, 202
Monster, grim, awful behaviour of, 160
Moon. *See* Dorsal region, lunar
Morals, Voltaire's, wound up by Dr. Young, 66
Mothers, brave men weep at mention of their, 232
Mountains, Welsh, frequented by goats and botanists, 82
Muse, reformed by a pension, 5; fooled by grovelling sons of verse, 73; the manurial, 91; invited to celebrate Mr. Baker's return to health, 109; proves unequal to the task, 110

Napoleon I, uncertainty as to his present whereabouts, 10
Nature, her sins commensurate with her size, xiv; a coy and aged virgin, 25; run to earth by Dr. Harvey, 26
Negroes, liable to worms, 91; prone to bloat, ibid.; their nails often found in Christmas puddings, 98
Newspaper editors, not always truthful, 240
Newt, trustworthy, 202
Nitrogen, discreet amours of, 108
Norns, reboantic, 185

Ocean, baffled by a pier, 11; a truly British theme, 67; pleasant when calm, otherwise when rough, 69
Owl, stuffed, emotions evoked by contemplation of, 151
Oxford Street, anapæstic extension of, 144
Oxygen, glorious, God's, xv
Oysters, when in season, 20; reason why they cannot be crossed in love, 108

Pales, gifts of. *See* Milk

Palmerston, Lord, obituary notice of, 229

Panegyrics upon Royal Personages, 9, 12, 38, *et passim*; upon Peeresses and Court Ladies, 10, 103–4; upon Mr. Philips (by Mr. Philips), 57; upon tadpoles, tapeworms, etc., 108

Parliament, British, strikes universal terror, 73; members of, the noblest offspring of the gods, 74; their mental repletion, 195

Pea, not self-supporting, 22

Phyllis, reprehended for not supporting home industries, 81

Pindar, not so fortunate as Dr. Young in his choice of theme, 73

Planets, mercantile activities of, 72

Pond, 3′ × 2′, 148; reader invited to visit it, ibid.

Prince Consort, his keen appreciation of scenery, 226; tearfully thanked for the Great Exhibition, 243

Property, a native of England, 55; its name inscribed on fruits of earth by Liberty, 92; secures the conscious swain, 93

Props, required by hops, 97

Railway locomotives, etiquette observed by, 195

Ram, services of hatter welcomed by, 77

Reynolds, Miss, a mass of beauty, 10

Rum, grateful strains inspired by, 8

Salt meat, easily thawed to chyle by athletic hinds, 61

Sand. *See* False Gallia's sons

Scorpions, a double handful of, 119

Sewage system, metropolitan, eulogised, 207

Shakespeare, quoted, 215; confuted, 216

Shark disposes of Bryan in two instalments, 89

Sheep, British, unhappy in exile, 81; urged by Colin to keep their wool on, ibid. *See also* Bleaters

Shepherds, Spanish, effeminate habits of, 81

Silk-worm, Spartan tastes of, 150; sinks into hopeless grave, 152

Smile, Queen Mary's, its anticipated effect on national prosperity, 39; social, donned by rustic in leisure moments, 137. *See also* Corpse

Smith, Mr., and comfort share blood-stained tomb, 110

Smoke. *See* Incense of thanksgiving *and* Vapour, thundrous

Snail, domesticated, 150; affectionate, 171

Spade, so denominated, 1

Spoon, Time's, culinary employment of, by Life, 29

Spurs, worn on bare feet by Italian brigands, 206

State assistance to public companies, a reasoned scheme for, 224

Steamboat, regrettably flighty behaviour of, 151; a duck of a, 193

Stomach, languid, curses fat, 61

Stud-farms, essential to the Empire's continued existence, 232

Sugar. *See* Sand

Sun, obscured by Mr. Merry, 118

Surprise, vain, Samson's, 19; immense, Mr. Gunston's, 48; unqualified, Jonah's, 65

Swains, slow, 77; honest, 90; conscious, 93. *See also* Hinds

Tadpole, poetically celebrated, 108

Tænia. *See* Tapeworm

Tapeworm, lonely but prolific, 108

Tears, telescopic, 11; examples of their use in sundry emergencies, 139–40; miscellaneous, 6, 14, 22, 35, 70, 115, 122, 123, 137, 169, 227, 232

Thought, silent tickler of the human brain, 18

Trade, a native of Great Britain, 66; gingered up by Industry, 67; loftiest of poetic themes, 72; interplanetary, ibid.; snatched by Dr. Young from the shores of prose, ibid.

Trains, rapture of catching, 6; used indiscriminately by all ranks, 195

Truffle, love-lorn, 108

Umbrellas, their use by Highland crofters discommended, 151

Vapour, thundrous, emitted by steam-eagles, 188

Vegetable marrow, its richness and grandeur, 22

Victoria, Queen, makes a dash for Frogmore, 17

Wages, agricultural, uniform, 4

Walking-stick, address to a bereaved, 158

Warner, Mrs., goes house-hunting in heaven, 49

Washing, cautiously recommended, 62

Werter, a man of woe, 117; vacuum of his generous breast, how filled, 118

Wet-nurses, denounced, 96; male parents useless as, 153

Wickliff, John, an enterprising sage, 14

William III, his royal breach repaired, 17; escorted from Torbay by brigades of angels, 50

Wives should wash occasionally, 63; a modicum of intelligence desirable in, 158; but not too much, 211

Woman, useful as a protection against lions, 118

Workhouse, impassioned invitation to the, 78

Worm, lisping, 4; militant, 8; far-fetched, *see* Silk-worm

Yams, conflict of authorities concerning, 2

Yarker, Mr., his lamented dropping off, 216

York, Duke of, a cargo in himself, 31

INDEX OF AUTHORS

Addison, Joseph, 44–6

"Anna Matilda." *See* Cowley, Hannah

Anonymous, *and* Authors Unknown, 1, 3, 10, 12, 15, 16, 18, 21, 22, 23, 250

Armstrong, John, 60–3

Austin, Alfred, xiv, 2, 3, 4, 6, 7, 16, 20, 249, 250

Babu Poets, 11, 17

Bailey, Philip James, 22

Baker, T., 1, 6, 192–8

Balmford, William, 4

Banks, John, 33

Bayly, Thomas Haynes, 19, 166–70

Bewley, Samuel, 251

Bidlake, John, 22

Blackmore, Sir Richard, 3, 40–3

Blair, Robert, 250

Bloomfield, Robert, 8

Boyce, William, 18, 20

Brown, Solyman, 13

Brown, Thomas Edward, 1

Browning, Elizabeth Barrett, 3, 15, 18, 187–8

Browning, Robert, 2, 7

Buckinghamshire, Duke of, 36–7

Burns, Robert, 14, 114–15

Byron, Lord, 139–42

Campbell, Thomas, 15

Canfield, H. C., 11

Carnegie of Pitarrow, 16

Chapman, George, 14   [10

Chatterton, Thomas, xii, 109–

Chivers, Thomas Holley, 183–6

Cibber, Colley, 9, 51–4

Cleveland, John, 9

Close, John, 215–16

Coleridge, Samuel Taylor, 15

Collins, Mortimer, 19

Coogler, J. Gordon, 6

Cook, Eliza, 7, 199–203

Cottle, Joseph, 129–30

Courtenay, John, xii   [144

Cowley, Abraham, 5, 6, 24–6,

Cowley, Hannah, 121–3

Cowper, William, 4, 76

Crabbe, George, xii, 3, 16, 111–13, 242

Crashaw, Richard, 1

Darwin, Erasmus, 105–8

"Della Crusca." *See* Merry, Robert

Della Cruscans, 124–5

Dobell, Sydney Thompson, 217–18

Dryden, John, 5, 20, 30–2, 249

Duncombe, John, 102–4

Dyer, John, 76–9, 92

Elmore, James K., 19

Emerson, Ralph Waldo, 164–5

Eusden, Laurence, 9

Eveleigh, George, 224–5

Farmer, Edward, 14

Foot, Edwin Edward, 18, 226–9

Gay, John, 249

Girdlestone, E. D., 250

Goldsmith, Oliver, 99–101
Gordon, Adam Lindsay, xv, 230–2
Gould, Gerald, 250   [171
Grainger, James, 2, 5, 8, 87–91,

Hayley, William, 4
Hervey, Lord, 58–9
Hobbes, Thomas, 14
Hogg, James, 3
Hogg, Thomas, 9
Howitt, William, 20
Hunt, James Henry Leigh, 1, 5, 15, 132–5
Hymnodists, 4, 8, 19, 20, 250

Jerningham, Edward, 94–6
Johnson, Samuel, xi, 4

Keats, John, 153–4

Llewellyn, Evan, 22
Longfellow, Henry Wadsworth, 189–91
Lytton, Earl of, 2, 9, 171, 219–23

Mackay, Charles, 177–9
Mackay, Eric, xv, 6
Maginn, William, 16
Meredith, George, xv, 5
"Meredith, Owen." *See* Lytton, Earl of
Merry, Robert, 116–20
Montgomery, Robert, 7, 173–6
Moore, Julia, 10, 233–41

Newcastle, Duchess of, 27–9
Nichols, John. 14

Parsons, William, 125
Poe, Edgar Allan, 180–2
Pollok, Robert, 162–3
Pomfret, John, 6, 11

Robinson, Mary, 126–8
Rossetti, Dante Gabriel, 12
Ruskin, John, 14

Scott, John, of Amwell, xii, 12
Scott, Sir Walter, 249
Seward, Thomas, 7
Shadwell, Thomas, 17
Shenstone, William, 2, 15, 80–4
Smart, Christopher, 97–8
Smith, Alexander, 1, 8, 17
Smith, Elizabeth Oakes, 171–2
Southey, Robert, 131
Sprat, Thomas, 34–5
Stedman, William Nathan, 16
Steele, Sir Richard, 2
Sternhold, Thomas, and Hopkins, John, 15

T., Mr., 21
Tate, Nahum, 38–9
Tennyson, Lord, xv, 2, 8, 11, 18, 242–8, 249
Tupper, Martin Farquhar, 2, 208–14
Turner, Elizabeth, 4

University Poets, 2, 17

Vaughan, Henry, 1

Waddington, George, 13
Waller, Edmund, 3
Warton, Joseph, 85–6
Warton, Thomas, 92–3
Watts, Isaac, 6, 11, 47–50, 109
Wesley, Charles, 18, 21
White, Henry Kirke, 136–8
Whur, Cornelius, 155–61
Wilcox, Ella Wheeler, 13
Wordsworth, William, xii, 1, 14, 16, 17, 21, 143–52, 249, 251
Young, Edward, 5, 7, 12, 64–75

DATE DUE

MAR 28 '68			
AUG 15 1972			
GAYLORD			PRINTED IN U.S.A.